Mastering Arab

Activity Book
Intermediate Level Practice

Jane Wightwick &
Mahmoud Gaafar

HIPPOCRENE BOOKS, INC.
New York

Hippocrene Books, Inc. edition, 2016.

First published in English by Palgrave, a division of Macmillan Publishers Limited under the title *Mastering Arabic 2 Activity Book* edited by Jane Wightwick and Mahmoud Gaafar. This edition has been published under license from Palgrave. The authors have asserted their right to be identified as the author of this Work.

ISBN 13: 978-0-7818-1350-1

Cataloging-in-Publication data available from the Library of Congress.

For more information, contact:
HIPPOCRENE BOOKS, INC.
171 Madison Avenue
New York, NY 10016
www.hippocrenebooks.com.

Printed in China.

Photo credits
The authors and publishers wish to acknowledge the following sources, with thanks for permission to reproduce photographs and illustrations:
Shutterstock: Zurijeta, p6; Shots Studio, p17; Rahhal, p46; Pavel L. Photo and Video, p47; Zurijeta, p70; Fotalia: Anna Omelchenko, p12; Robert Kneschke, p52; philipus, p64; wckiw, p66; 123RF: Jergen Schaetzke, p20; nisanga, p22; Sompop U-kong, p48; iStock: Zurijeta, p80.

Contents

Acknowledgements

We would like to thank Taoufiq Cherkaoui (Arabic and Islamic Education Coordinator, Dubai British School), Saussan Khalil (Faculty of Asian and Middle Eastern Studies, University of Cambridge), and Najwa Kadhim (King's College London), who reviewed the activities in this book. The encouragement and valuable comments provided by these experienced Arabic teachers have made an important contribution to the book.

As always, we are indebted to the continuing support of the team at Macmillan Education, Palgrave, particularly our long-standing and unfailingly enthusiastic publisher, Helen Bugler.

Introduction

Mastering Arabic 2: Activity Book has been developed to provide lively and enjoyable additional practice for intermediate students of Arabic, whether learning by yourself or within a group. The carefully graded activities will reinforce vocabulary and concepts in a variety of ways and so increase confidence and understanding as you progress in your study of Arabic.

Mastering Arabic 2: Activity Book is especially suitable for use alongside the leading Arabic language course, *Mastering Arabic 2*, providing learners with additional practice at intermediate level, as well as at beginner level. The activities have been designed to complement the 14 units of the main course. The vocabulary and structures used in *Mastering Arabic 2: Activity Book* are also taken directly from the main course and reworked to provide reinforcement. However, *Mastering Arabic 2: Activity Book* is also very useful for others wishing to improve their Arabic, and does not rely on knowledge of the main course.

The *Mastering Arabic* series teaches the universally understood Modern Standard Arabic. As in the main course, however, whenever there are dialogues or situations in which the colloquial language would naturally be used, we have tried to choose vocabulary and structures that are as close as possible to the spoken form.

How to use *Mastering Arabic 2: Activity Book*

You can use *Mastering Arabic 2: Activity Book* to reinforce your learning as you go along, or as a review before you move on to a higher level. The answers at the back of the book will help you to assess your progress. Try to revisit areas about which you feel uncertain. Then go back and try the activities again.

Mastering Arabic website

Next to some of the activities you will find the website symbol above. This indicates that there is additional material to accompany *Mastering Arabic 2: Activity Book* on the series website (www.palgrave.com/masteringarabic). The additional material is in the form of further ideas for extension activities, enlarged versions of crosswords, and model examples for the final practice at the end of each unit.

You will also find a wealth of other resources on the series website to help you with your study of Arabic, including audio flashcards, extra worksheets, reference material and videos.

1 Myself and others
أنا والآخَرون

1 Complete the sentences with the correct family members according to the description of the relationship. Include هو (he) or هي (she) as appropriate. The first is an example.

١   أمّ أبي...   **هي جَدَّتي** _____

٢   أخو أبي... _____

٣   أبو زوجي... _____

٤   أخت أمّي... _____

٥   أمّ زوجتي... _____

٦   ابن ابنتي... _____

٧   أبو أمّي... _____

٨   ابنة ابني... _____

٩   أخو أمّي... _____

١٠ أخت أبي... _____

2 Choose an adjective from the box to describe each characteristic and write it below the picture, as in the example.

وفيّ	عنيد	ذكيّ	موهوب
حكيم	مكّار	محبوب	رشيق
مُضحِك	كريم	نشيط	رقيق

ـــــــــ ٤ ـــــــــ ٣ ـــــــــ ٢ **١ رشيق**

ـــــــــ ٨ ـــــــــ ٧ ـــــــــ ٦ ـــــــــ ٥

ـــــــــ ١٢ ـــــــــ ١١ ـــــــــ ١٠ ـــــــــ ٩

3 Using ‫...‬إنّ ولكنّ ‫...‬ , how would you say the following in Arabic ?

My granddaughter is talented but she's stubborn. ١

_____

My (paternal) aunt's husband is poor but he's very generous. ٢

_____

My (female) friend is clever and popular but she's a little lazy. ٣

_____

Majid is at the police station. The police officer is attempting to fill in a form with his details. From the conversation, fill in the information on the form. What piece of information is missing, and what irrelevant piece of information does Majid give the officer?

الشرطيّ: ما اسمك؟

ماجد: اسمي ... اسمي ... اسمي ... ماجد.

الشرطيّ: ماجد فقط؟

ماجد: نعم، اسمي ماجد فقط.

الشرطيّ: لا، لا. ما اسم العائلة؟

ماجد: آه! فهمت الآن! اسمي ماجد محمّد محفوظ.

الشرطيّ: وأنت من أين؟

ماجد: أنا أصلاً من الأقصر.

الشرطيّ: عظيم. وأين تُقيم الآن؟

ماجد: أُقيم مع جدّتي.

الشرطيّ: ولكن يا ماجد، أنا لا أعرف أين تُقيم جدّتك.

ماجد: أنا أعرف عُنوانها!

الشرطيّ: هل أنت مهرّج يا ماجد؟

ماجد: نعم! نعم! كيف عرفتَ مِهنتي؟!

الاسم ....

اسم العائلة ....

العنوان ....

الجنسية ....

المهنة ....

5 Rewrite the personal information below to refer to the subject in brackets, as in the example.

١ أنا اسمي ماجد. (هو) ___ **هو اسمه ماجد.** _____

٢ هل أنتَ لبنانيّ؟ (أنتُم) _____

٣ عندنا كلب أسود. (هُم) _____

٤ عُنواني ٤٥ شارع النهر. (هي) _____

٥ أخي موهوب ولكنَّه كسول. (أختي) _____

٦ كان لِعمّي شقّة كبيرة. (نحن) _____

٧ أبي كان طبيب أسنان. (أمّي) _____

٨ أمضى أحمد طُفولته هنا. (أنا) _____

٩ إنّ حماتي فقيرة ولكنّها كريمة. (حمي)

_____

6 Join the two halves of the sentences, for example: ج ١.

أ هو ابن أختي نادية.	١ هذا الرجل غنيّ الآن، ولكن...
ب ولكن خالي عنده كلب أسود.	٢ نعيش في ألمانيا منذ سنوات...
ت وتغنّي في كلّ حفلات المدرسة.	٣ أنا خال هذا الولد الصغير...
ث لأنها نشيطة ومحبوبة وكريمة.	٤ ابنتي الكبيرة موهوبة ...
ج عائلته كانت فقيرة.	٥ يُقيم جدّي في نفس المكان...
ح في شقّته الصغيرة بجوار النهر.	٦ خالتي عندها قطّة بيضاء...
خ ونقيم في قرية قريبة من برلين.	٧ كلّ الحيّ يعرف جدّتي ياسمين...

Ibrahim has written a short introduction about himself. Read the text and complete the English translation below.

Tip: مَزرَعة = farm; مُساعِد = assistant.

أنا اسمي إبراهيم الخليجيّ
وأنا كويتيّ، أصلاً من الوَفرة
في جنوب الكويت.

وُلِدتُ في عام ١٩٩٠ وعندي أخ واحد وثلاث
أخَوات. قَبلَ عشرين سنة، أبي كان له
مَزرَعة في الوفرة وأمضيتُ طُفولتي هناك.
أُقيم الآن في الدوحة، عاصمة قطر،
وأنا مُساعِد المُدير في فندق كبير.
إنّي مشغول جدًّا ولكنّي سعيد!

My name's Ibrahim _____ and I'm _____ ,
originally from Al-Wafra in the _____ of _____ .

I was _____ in the year 1990 and _____ one
brother and _____ _____ . Twenty years ago,
my _____ had a _____ in Wafra and I spent my
_____ there.

I now live in Doha, the _____ of _____ , and
I'm the _____ manager in a large _____ .

I'm very _____ but I'm _____ .

8 ● **Talk about it yourself**   تَكَلّم عَنها بِنَفسك

Now imagine your name is Jamil (if you are male) or Jamila (if you are female). Write an introduction about yourself, using Ibrahim's paragraph on page 6 as a model, and replacing his details with the information below:

- Your family name is Mansour (منصور).
- You are Lebanese, from Halba (حلبا) in the north of Lebanon.
- You were born in 1989.
- You have three brothers and one sister.
- Twenty-five years ago, your father had a bakery in Halba.
- You now live in Cairo, and work as assistant to the chef in a small restaurant.
- You are very happy but poor!

Make sure you adjust the text to the feminine if you're female.

When you've finished, check your answer with the model on the website.

_____

_____

_____

_____

_____

_____

_____

_____

_____

Finish by writing another introduction based on your real details, perhaps also recording it as speaking practice.

Unit 2 — House and home
الدار والبيت

1 Write the names of the rooms or outdoor features next to the correct numbers, as in the example.

٦ _____		سطح _____	١
٧ _____		_____	٢
٨ _____		_____	٣
٩ _____		_____	٤
١٠ _____		_____	٥

2 Now say in which room or outdoor feature of the house you would find these items, as in the example.

١ سيّارة <u>سَتَجِد السيّارة في الجراج.</u>

٢ سرير _____

٣ أريكة _____

٤ فُرن _____

٥ دُش _____

٦ مائدة الطَعام _____

٧ سُلَّم _____

٨ عُشب _____

3 What are the plurals and meanings of these words related to the home? Write them after the singular, as in the example.

٩ كرسيّ _____	١ حَمّام <u>حمّامات</u> *bathrooms*
١٠ شَقّة _____	٢ بيت _____
١١ شُرفة _____	٣ غُرفة _____
١٢ ساعة _____	٤ حَوض _____
١٣ سَطح _____	٥ مَطبَخ _____
١٤ مَنزِل _____	٦ فُرن _____
١٥ مائدة _____	٧ مِصعَد _____
١٦ مَدخَل _____	٨ ثَلاجة _____

4 Sanya is looking for someone to undertake a few jobs around her luxury villa. An internet search has thrown up these three local companies.

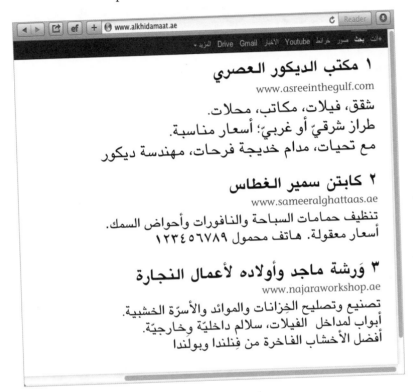

Decide which company you feel would be most suitable for each of Sanya's jobs, as listed below.

	٣	٢	١
a Fix broken chair in the dining room	✔		
b Redesign study in traditional Eastern style			
c Clean out fish tanks in hall			
d Choose new curtains for main bedroom			
e Repair entrance door and stairs			
f Redecorate the living room			
g Build wardrobe in Sara's bedroom			
h Undertake annual swimming pool clean			

5 Now find these Arabic words and expressions in the search listing and decide what they mean, as in the example.

١ أحواض السمك _____ *fish tanks* _____

٢ تَصنيع وتَصليح _____

٣ أسعار معقولة _____

٤ طِراز شرقيّ أو غربيّ _____

٥ مهندسة ديكور _____

٦ سلالم داخليّة وخارجيّة _____

٧ تَنظيف حمامات السباحة _____

٨ أفضل الأخشاب الفاخرة _____

6 In the end, Sanya has decided to commission one single service company to undertake all of the jobs. She is showing the service manager around the villa and pointing out what needs to be done. Complete her brief to match the list of jobs in Activity 4.

في الصالة، نحتاج إلى تنظيف أحواض (١) **السمك** . وفي المدخل، نحتاج إلى تصليح (٢) _____ والسلّم الداخليّ. كما نحتاج إلى تصليح (٣) _____ المكسور في غرفة الطعام وتجديد ديكور (٤) _____ المعيشة. أما في الطابق الأوّل، فنريد تصنيع خزانة في غرفة ابنتنا، سارة، و(٥) _____ جديدة لغرفتنا، وأيضاً تصميم (٦) _____ بالطراز (٧) _____ التقليديّ. وأخيراً، نريد تنظيف (٨) _____ السباحة.

7 Samira wants to move to a larger apartment. Read about her requirements and fill in the comparison chart below.

Tip: بـالإضـافة إلى = in addition to; غرفة الضُيوف = guest room.

> أنا أُقيم الآن في شقّة صغيرة في وسط المدينة.
>
> أنا أريد أن أبيع شقّتي لأشتري شقّة أكبر منها خارج المدينة.
>
> عندنا الآن غرفة نوم واحدة، ونحتاج إلى غرفة نوم ثانية لابنتي الصغيرة، داليا.
>
> بالإضافة إلى غرفة المعيشة، نريد غرفة للضيوف.
>
> شقّتي الآن في الطابق الرابع، ولكنّني لا أريد أن أشتري شقّة عاليَة. أفضّل شقّة في الطابق الأرضيّ لها حديقة خاصّة أو شرفة واسعة تلعب فيها داليا مع أصدقائها.
>
> يجب أن يكون سعرها مناسباً.

	Current apartment	Future apartment
Situation	middle of town	
Number of bedrooms		
Guest room		
Floor of apartment		
Garden/balcony		

8 🗨 **Talk about it yourself**   تَكَلَّم عَنها بِنَفسك

Now imagine you currently live in a large ground floor apartment outside town. You want to move to a smaller apartment in the middle of town.

You *don't* need:
- three bedrooms
- a private garden
- a guest room in addition to a living room

You *do* need:
- one large bedroom
- a flat on the second or third floor
- a lift and a small balcony

Using what Samira says on page 12 as a model, write about your current situation and your requirements for moving. When you have finished, check your answer with the model on the website.

_____

_____

_____

_____

_____

_____

_____

_____

_____

_____

Finish by describing the features of your own house or apartment, and any additional requirements you might have.

3 Work and routine
العَمَل والعادة

1 Arrange the letters and add the vowels to match the occupations, as in the example.

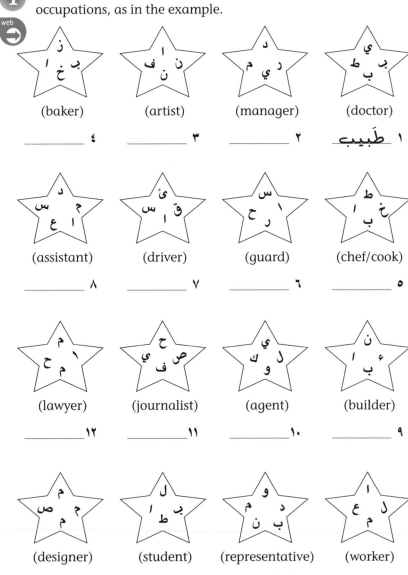

(baker)	(artist)	(manager)	(doctor)
٤ _____	٣ _____	٢ _____	١ <u>طَبيب</u>

(assistant)	(driver)	(guard)	(chef/cook)
٨ _____	٧ _____	٦ _____	٥ _____

(lawyer)	(journalist)	(agent)	(builder)
١٢ _____	١١ _____	١٠ _____	٩ _____

(designer)	(student)	(representative)	(worker)
١٦ _____	١٥ _____	١٤ _____	١٣ _____

2 Six of the occupations in Activity 1 *cannot* be made plural by adding ين/ون (-ūn/-īn). Identify these six occupations; then write each with its plural, as in the example.

طَبيب / أَطِبّاء (doctor/doctors) _____

_____

_____

_____

_____

3 Now read what different people have to say about their work and circle the occupation, as in the example.

١ عندي مخبز كبير في وسط المدينة.

نجّار / مهندس / خبّاز

٢ أعمل في جريدة اسمها «صَوت الناس».

ممرّضة / صحفيّة / محامية

٣ مطعمنا مشغول الليلة وكلّ الموائد محجوزة.

طلبة / محامون / طبّاخون

٤ رسمتُ لَوحة بالألوان لقصر الأميرة الجديد.

مدرّسة / فنّانة / حارسة

٥ عادةً لا نغادر المستشفى قبل الساعة العاشرة مساءً.

فنّانون / مغنّون / أَطِبّاء

٦ سأكون هنا الساعة الخامسة لأن المدير يريد أن يذهب إلى المطار.

سائق / مصمّم / بنّاء

4 A day in the life of Budur. Write the number of the picture that represents Budur's routine next to the correct caption below, as in the example.

☐ عادةً أقود سيّارتي إلى المخبز.

☐ كلّ يوم أستيقظ الساعة السادسة صباحاً.

☐ الساعة الخامسة، أرجع إلى منزلي وأطبخ العشاء لأُسرَتي.

☐ دائماً آكل الإفطار مع الشاي ولكنّي لا أشرب القهوة أبداً.

☐ في الصباح أنظّف الأرض في المخبز...

☐ بعد الدُش، أحياناً أكوي ملابس العمل.

١ أنا اسمي بُدور وأعمل في مخبر صغير.

☐ ...وأرتّب الكعك على الرَفّ.

5 You are telling a friend about Budur's routine. Fill in the missing words, as in the example.

هي اسمها بُدور و (١) **تعمل** ــــــ في مخبر صغير. كلّ يوم تستيقظ

بُدور الساعة (٢) ــــــ ـــــــ صباحاً. دائماً (٣) ـــــــ الإفطار

مع الشاي ولكنّها لا تشرب القهوة (٤) ـــــــ. بعد الدُش،

أحياناً (٥) ـــــــ ملابس العمل. عادةً تقود (٦) ـــــــ

إلى المخبز. في الصباح (٧) ـــــــ الأرض في المخبز و

(٨) ـــــــ الكعك. تعمل حتّى الساعة الخامسة، ثمّ ترجع إلى

(٩) ـــــــ و (١٠) ـــــــ العشاء لأُسرَتها.

6 Tareq is talking about his background and experience.

Tip: أجمَعُ = I collect; لَوحَات = paintings; رَغم أن = even though;
تَخَرَّجتُ = I graduated.

أنا اسمي طارق أبو زيد، وولدتُ
في عام ١٩٨٠. أنا تونسيّ، وأقيم في
مدينة بنزرت، ٤٤ شارع الميناء.
أنا وكيل للفنّانين التونسيّين،
وأجمع لَوحاتهم وصُوَرهم لأعرضها
وأبيعها في معارض كثيرة في أوروبا والشرق الأوسط.
أوّل وظيفة لي كانت في المتحف الثقافيّ سنة
٢٠٠٢، وبعد ثلاث سنوات تركتُ المتحف وقرّرتُ أن
أعمل وحدي رغم أنني كنتُ صغير السِنّ.
درستُ إدارة الأعمال في ميلانو وتخرّجتُ بتَقدير
'ممتاز'، ثمّ حصلتُ على شهادة في التصميم
بالكمبيوتر من جامعة ليدز في شمال إنجلترا.
أنا أتحدّث الإنجليزيّة والفرنسيّة بطَلاقة،
ومتوسّط في الإيطاليّة.

Now identify these Arabic words and phrases from the text,
and match them to their English equivalents, for example **a٦**.

a business administration	١ لأعرضها وأبيعها	
b the museum of culture	٢ الشرق الأوسط	
c with 'Excellent' grade	٣ المتحف الثقافيّ	
d the Middle East	٤ أعمل وحدي	
e I [would] work for myself	٥ كنتُ صغير السنّ	
f I speak ... fluently	٦ إدارة الأعمال	
g to show and sell them	٧ بتقدير 'ممتاز'	
h I was young	٨ تصميم بالكمبيوتر	
i computer-aided design	٩ أنا أتحدّث ... بطلاقة	

7 Fill in the missing details on Tareq's CV, using his description on page 17, as in the example.

السيرة الذاتية

الاسم: طارق أبو زيد ـــــ   الجِنس: ذكر

تاريخ الميلاد: ١٥/٦/ ـــــــــ   الجنسيّة: ـــــــــ

العُنوان: ٤٤ شارع ـــــــــ ، بنزرت

المُؤَهّلات:

كلّية إدارة ـــــــــ، جامعة ميلانو – التقدير: ـــــــــ

ـــــــــ ليدز – شهادة في ـــــــــ بالكمبيوتر

الخِبرة العمليّة:

٢٠٠٥ – : وكيل ـــــــــ (في الشرق ـــــــــ وأوروبا)

٢٠٠٢–٢٠٠٥: مساعد المدير، ـــــــــ الثقافيّ

المَهارات:

اللغة الإنجليزيّة: جيِّد جدًّا؛ اللغة الفرنسيّة: ـــــــــ جدًّا

اللغة الإيطاليّة: ـــــــــ

Talk about it yourself تكَلّم عَنها بِنَفسك

Here is the CV of a Lebanese journalist, May Malouf.

Use the information to write a description of May's background and experience, using Tareq's description on page 17 as a model.

When you have finished, check your answer with the model on the website.

Finish by writing another CV and description based on your real details.

السِيرة الذاتية

الاسم: ميّ معلوف   الجِنس: أنثى

تاريخ الميلاد: ١٩٨٥/١٠/٢٣   الجنسيَّة: لبنانيّة

العُنوان: ٦٥ شارع القلعة، بيروت

المُؤَهّلات:

كلّية اللغات، جامعة باريس – التقدير: ممتاز

المعهد العربيّ، بيروت – شهادة في الصحافة

الخِبرة العمليّة:

٢٠١٠ – : مراسلة للشرق الأوسط، محطّة TV5

٢٠٠٩–٢٠٠٧: سكرتيرة، جريدة «الأيّام»

المَهارات:

اللغة الفرنسيّة: جيّد جدًّا

اللغة الإنجليزيّة: متوسّط

_____

_____

_____

_____

_____

_____

_____

_____

_____

_____

_____

_____

_____

_____

unit 4 Sport and leisure
الرياضة والترفيه

web

1 Write the names of the sports in the box under the correct symbols, as in the example.

الكرة الطائِرة	الجولف	كرة اليَد	السِباحة
رُكوب الدرّاجات	تنس الطاوِلة	التنس	المُلاكَمة
كرة السَلّة	كرة القَدَم	ألعاب القُوَى	رُكوب الخَيل

٣ ــــــــــــــ   ٢ ــــــــــــــ   ١ ــ الجولف

٦ ــــــــــــــ   ٥ ــــــــــــــ   ٤ ــــــــــــــ

٩ ــــــــــــــ   ٨ ــــــــــــــ   ٧ ــــــــــــــ

١٢ ــــــــــــــ   ١١ ــــــــــــــ   ١٠ ــــــــــــــ

2 Now complete these two-word sports, as in the example.

٥ ــــــــــ اليد		١ ــــــــــ __كرة__ القدم
٦ ــــــــــ السمك		٢ ــــــــــ الطائرة
٧ ــــــــــ الدّراجات		٣ ــــــــــ الخيل
٨ ــــــــــ القُوى		٤ ــــــــــ الطاولة

3 Identify the meaning and root letters of these words related to sport and leisure, as in the example.

Root letters	Meaning	Word
ش/ه/د	viewing/watching	مُشاهَدة
		مَلعَب
		رُكوب
		تَصوير
		مُلاكَمة
		مُدرِّب
		سِباحة
		مُمتِع
		لاعِبون
		مُفَضَّل
		مُلاكِم
		ألعاب

4 Below is an advertisement for a sports and leisure club. Tick the facilities that are mentioned as being offered by the club.

Tip: الرَشاقة = suppleness/grace; غُروب الشَمس = sunset.

نادي النشاط العائلي

ملاعب فاخرة تطلّ على الشاطئ!

• تنس • جولف • اسكواش • كرة السلّة

تمرينات للرشاقة لكلّ العائلة!

أنشطة للأولاد في حدائق النادي!

ركوب الخيل على الشاطئ عند غُروب الشمس!

مطاعم هادئة ومريحة!

أهلاً بكم في أيّ وقت!

☐ كرة السلّة	☐ كرة القدم
☐ السباحة	☐ كرة اليد
☐ ركوب الدرّاجات	☐ الجولف
☐ الاسكواش	☐ تمرينات رياضيّة
☐ أنشطة عائليّة	☐ مطاعم
☐ إصطبلات	☐ صيد السمك
☐ الكرة الطائرة	☐ ملاعب تنس

Look at the chart below showing which sports are enjoyed by Marwan, his wife Ines and their son Kamal. The faces show whether each member of the family is positive (☺), negative (☹) or neutral (😐) about a sport.

☺	😐	😐	☺	☹	😐	☺	مروان
☺	☹	☹	😐	☺	☺	☹	إيناس
☺	😐	☺	☺	☹	☺	😐	كمال

Now decide who is expressing each of the opinions below, as in the example.

١ أحبّ أن أشاهد الجولف لأنّه ممتع. ــــــ مروان ــــــ

٢ لا أحبّ الملاكمة إطلاقاً بسبب العُنف. ــــــ

٣ نحن نحبّ كرة السلّة لأنّها مسلّية. ــــــ

٤ أكره الجولف وتنس الطاولة. ــــــ

٥ لا أهتمّ بكرة السلّة؛ أفضّل كرة القدم. ــــــ

٦ ركوب الخيل مثير وأحبّه كثيراً! ــــــ

٧ أمّا الجولف، فأنا أكره هذه الرياضة. ــــــ

٨ نحن لا نحبّ ركوب الخيل لأنّه مملّ. ــــــ

٩ لا أهتمّ بمشاهدة كرة القدم. ــــــ

١٠ نحن نشاهد ألعاب القوى دائماً! ــــــ

6 Ines is complaining about how Marwan likes to watch golf on the television. Read the text and complete the English translation below.

زوجي مروان يحبّ أن يشاهد الجولف على التليفزيون . أنا لا أستطيع أن أشاهد أكثر من خمس دَقائِق، ثمّ أنام على الأريكة! أنا لا أفهَم كيف يشاهد هذه الرياضة المملّة لمدّة ساعة، أو ساعتَين، أو حتّى ثلاث ساعات . الكرة صغيرة جدّاً، واللاعبون يمشون ببُطءٍ شديد .

لا شيءَ مُمتِع . لا لَحظة مُثيرة . إنّها رياضة مُناسِبة لأيّ شخص لا يستطيع أن ينام . هذه هي فائِدتها الوحيدة!

My _____ Marwan _____ to watch

_____ on the TV. I can't _____ for more than

_____ minutes, then I fall asleep on the _____ !

I don't _____ how he can watch this _____

sport for an hour, or _____ hours, or even _____

hours. The ball is very _____ , and the _____

walk extremely slowly.

There's nothing _____ . Not one _____ moment.

It's a _____ suitable for someone who can't

_____ . That is its only _____ !

Talk about it yourself تَكَلَّم عَنْها بِنَفْسِك

Now write a paragraph about sports and leisure activities, using the phrases you have practised in this unit. Follow these summary points in your paragraph:

- You go to the club on Friday.
- You like basketball and squash a lot. They're very exciting.
- You don't mind golf, but you really don't like football. You think it's boring.
- You like horse riding, but you don't like watching it on TV.
- Your father likes to watch boxing, but you hate it because of the violence. You can't watch it for more than five minutes.
- You prefer athletics. They're enjoyable.

When you've finished, check your answer with the model on the website.

_____

_____

_____

_____

_____

_____

_____

_____

_____

Finish by writing another paragraph based on your real preferences, perhaps also recording it as speaking practice.

5 Travel and tourism
السَفَر والسِياحة

1 Match the places around town to their English equivalents, for example ١e.

a post office

b shopping centre

c train station

d tourist office

e police station

f bus station

g sports centre

h airline office

i petrol station

١ مَركَز الشُرطة

٢ مَحَطّة القِطار

٣ مَكتَب الطَيران

٤ مَركَز التَسَوُّق

٥ مَحَطّة البَنزين

٦ مَكتَب البَريد

٧ مَكتَب السِياحة

٨ مَحَطّة الباص

٩ مَركَز الرِياضة

2 These people are either going to, or coming from, one of the destinations above. Write down which it is, as in the example.

١ رجل ومعهُ خطابات وبطاقات بريديّة. ‏مَكتَب البَريد

٢ سيّدة ومعها أكياس وفستان جديد. _____

٣ ولد ومعهُ مِضرَب تنس وحقيبة. _____

٤ سيّدة ومعها صورة اللصّ وهو يجري. _____

٥ رجل ومعهُ تذكرة ومَواعيد القطارات. _____

٦ أمريكيّ يلبَس شورت، ويسأل عن المتحف. _____

3 Complete the sentences below using the means of transportation illustrated, as in the example.

(Yesterday, I went to the fort ...) ... أمس ذهبتُ إلى القَلعة

_____ ٣   _____ ٢   ١ **بالباص** *(by bus)*

_____ ٦   _____ ٥   _____ ٤

_____ ٩   _____ ٨   _____ ٧

4 Now decide which means of transportation is *not* appropriate for the following people and circle it, as in the example.

Tip: نُقود = cash; رُخصة القِيادة = driving licence.

قطار / طائرة / مركب   ١ زوجي لا يُحبّ الطيران أبداً.

سيّارة / قطار / جمل   ٢ ابنَتي تخاف من الحَيَوانات.

باص / دَرّاجة / قطار الأنفاق   ٣ لا نعرِف كيف نركَب الدَرّاجات.

سَفينة / طائرة / حِمار   ٤ أشعُر بالمَرض على المَراكِب.

سيّارة / باص / مركب   ٥ رُخصة القِيادة ليسَت معي.

ماشياً / دَرّاجة / تاكسي   ٦ ليس معي أيّ نُقود.

5 Join the two halves of the sentences, for example: ت١.

أ لأنّك شاهدتَ السَرِقة؟		١ نَذهب إلى محطّة البنزين...
ب لتَستَقبِل مدير الشَركة.		٢ أنا أبحَث عن محطّة الباص...
ت لأنّنا نَحتاج إلى البنزين.		٣ هل كنتَ في مركز الشرطة...
ث لأنّهُ يريد أن يسافر إلى لَندُن.		٤ كانوا في مكتب السياحة...
ج لأشتري ملابس جديدة.		٥ سارة كانت في محطّة القطار...
ح لأذهب إلى وسط المدينة.		٦ أبي سيذهب إلى مكتب الطيران...
خ لأنّهم يحتاجون إلى خريطة.		٧ سأذهب إلى مركز التسوّق اليوم...

6 Identify the meaning and root letters of these verbs in the past, as in the example.

Root letters	Meaning	Verb
م/ش/ي	I walked	مَشَيْتُ
		شَعَرَتْ
		زُرْتُم
		نِمْتِ
		لَم يُغادِروا
		وَقَفْتُ
		أعَدّوا
		لم أجِد
		حَلَّ
		اِشْتَرَتْ

7 Rewrite the sentences and questions below to refer to the past, as in the example.

١ يَذهَب سمير إلى الجامعة بالباص.

ذَهَبَ سمير إلى الجامعة بالباص.

٢ سنَركَب المركب إلى ميناء جدّة.

_____

٣ الرحلة مُمتِعة ومُثيرة جدّاً.

_____

٤ هل تَشعُرين بالعصبيّة على الطائرة؟

_____

٥ أذهَب إلى السينما القريبة من بيتي.

_____

٦ سيزورون أحمد في شقّته الجديدة.

_____

٧ يقِف الأسد ورائي، ولكنّي لا أشعُر بالخَوف.

_____

٨ نمشي إلى الواحة ولكنّنا لا نشرَب الماء من البئر.

_____

٩ هل ستُعِدّون الحقائب وتشتَرون التذاكر؟

_____

8 Last summer Fadi went with a tourist group on a two-day trip to the Moroccan desert. Use the picture prompts to complete the description of his journey, as in the example.

Tip: Think about whether you need to add the extra *alif tanwin* (اً) to the missing word when it directly follows a verb.

في الصَيف الماضي سافرتُ مع مَجموعة سياحيّة إلى المغرب.

سافرنا إلى مدينة مرّاكش بالـ(١) _____ ،

ونزلنا في فندق صغير. كان في الفندق حديقة جميلة فيها

(٢) _____ بألوان كثيرة.

الساعة السادسة والنصف صباحاً، غادرنا الفندق وركبنا

الـ(٣) _____ لنذهب إلى وادي «تودغا» في

الصحراء. في الطريق، شاهدنا (٤) _____ عجيبة.

زُرنا واحة خضراء جميلة، وجلسنا تحت (٥) _____

وشربنا من ماء الـ(٦) _____ . كان مُنعِشاً جدّاً.

في المساء، تَوَجَّهنا نحو قَرية بدويّة صغيرة. أنا ركبتُ

(٧) _____ ، ومشيتُ بين كُثبان الرمل، ولكنّي كنتُ

عصبياً جدّاً وأنا فوق الجمل. نِمتُ في (٨) _____

وشاهدتُ (٩) _____ كثيرة لامعة في سَماء الليل.

في الفجر غادرنا القرية لنرجع إلى مرّاكش. في الطريق، شاهدنا

(١٠) _____ قديمة وعجيبة. ذَكَّرَتني بالأفلام القديمة.

بعد الغداء، رجعنا إلى مراكش. كانت رحلة مُمتِعة جدّاً!

Talk about it yourself   تَكَلَّم عَنها بِنَفسك

Now imagine that last winter you went on a two-day tour of the
Omani desert with a tourist group.
- You travelled to the city of Muscat by plane.
- You stayed in a large hotel; there was a garden with a lot of
  beautiful tall palm trees.
- At dawn, you headed towards the mountains and the desert.
- On the way, you saw an amazing old fort.
- You arrived at an oasis and ate dinner under the stars.
- You slept in a tent between the sand dunes.
- The next day, you left to go back to Muscat. On the way,
  you visited a small Bedouin village.

Using Fadi's description on page 30 as a model, write about your journey.
When you've finished, check your answer with the model on the website.

_____

_____

_____

_____

_____

_____

_____

_____

_____

Finish by describing a memorable journey of your own. Include the
places you visited and some of the things you saw and did.

6 Food and cooking
الطَعام والطَبخ

1 Write the Arabic for these foods alongside their English equivalents, as in the example.

_____	onions ١٠	دَجاج	chicken ١
_____	meat ١١	_____	cheese ٢
_____	water ١٢	_____	bananas ٣
_____	mint ١٣	_____	juice ٤
_____	butter ١٤	_____	garlic ٥
_____	dates ١٥	_____	fish ٦
_____	carrots ١٦	_____	bread ٧
_____	figs ١٧	_____	cucumber ٨
_____	rice ١٨	_____	eggs ٩

2 Now decide which one of the three foods listed is the odd one out and circle it, as in the example.

٥ ماء / بصل / عصير

١ جبن / حليب / طماطم

٦ كعك / بسكويت / سمك

٢ برتقال / ثوم / موز

٧ جزر / بنّ / شاي

٣ لحم / دجاج / خبز

٨ زبدة / خيار / طماطم

٤ تين / بطاطس / أرزّ

3 How much of each food do you want? Look at the picture prompts and ask for the quantities, as in the example.

١   [image] ١ + [image] = أريد كيلو لحم. _____

٢   [image] + [image] = _____

٣   [image] + [image] = _____

٤   [image] ½ + [image] = _____

٥   [image] + [image] = _____

٦   [image] ١٠٠ + [image] = _____

٧   [image] + [image] = _____

4 Arrange these food items in order of cost, from the cheapest to the most expensive. The cheapest is done for you as an example.

☐ كيلو اللحم بثلاثين جنيه في كلّ محلات الجزارة.

☐ هل كيلو التفّاح بعشرة جنيهات؟

☐ كيلو الليمون هنا بنصف جنيه.

☐ اشتريتُ ١٠٠ جرام بُنّ يَمَنيّ بأربعة جنيهات أمس.

☐ كيلو الطماطم بخمسة جنيهات اليوم.

١ كيلو السكّر عندهم بربع جنيه.

☐ كيلو المنجا بعشرين جنيه عند سليمان الخُضَري.

☐ عندنا بطاطس، الكيلو بجنيه.

الطبق الأوّل

١ ليمون مخلّل أو جزر مخلّل

٢ سلاطة الزبادي مع ثوم ونعناع مقطّع

٣ وَرَق عِنَب محشيّ باللحم المفروم

٤ سلاطة الحمّص بالكمّون وزيت الزيتون

الطبق الرئيسيّ

٥ لحم ضأني في الفرن مع البصل والثوم

٦ كفتة (أسياخ لحم مفروم)، مشويّة على الفحم

٧ دجاج مقليّ مع بطاطس مهروسة بالزبدة

٨ سمك مشويّ مع بطاطس محمّرة

٩ سلاطة العَدس مع بيض مسلوق وجزر مبشور

١٠ بيتزا (طماطم وجبن وزيتون)

الحلويات

١٤ سلاطة الفواكه ١١ تمر محشيّ باللوز

١٥ بطّيخ ١٢ أرزّ بالحليب

١٣ كعك تقليديّ بالقِشدة

المشروبات

١٩ عصير منجا ١٦ شاي بالنعناع

٢٠ عصير برتقال ١٧ حليب بالشوكولاتة

٢١ كولا ١٨ قهوة عربيّة

Tip: عَدس = lentils; وَرَق عِنَب = vine leaves; قِشدة = cream.

5 Look at the restaurant menu opposite. Pick out the Arabic for these dishes, which appear on the menu, and write them next to their English equivalents, as in the example.

_____ تمر محشيّ _____ stuffed dates ١

_____ mashed potatoes ٢

_____ grated carrot ٣

_____ minced meat skewers ٤

_____ pickled lemons ٥

_____ traditional cake ٦

_____ chickpea salad ٧

_____ stuffed vine leaves ٨

_____ boiled eggs ٩

_____ chopped mint ١٠

6 Now decide which dishes and drinks on the menu are _unsuitable_ for these customers with particular requirements. Write the numbers of the unsuitable items on the menu. The first one has been started for you.

_____ ٣، ٥، _____ vegetarian (no meat or fish) ١

_____ caffeine intolerant ٢

_____ lactose intolerant (no milk products) ٣

_____ allergic to pulses (lentils, etc.) and nuts ٤

_____ allergic to eggs and chocolate ٥

_____ plain eater (no mint, garlic or olives) ٦

Najwa and Farida have met up for lunch at a local restaurant.
Read their conversation with the *maitre d'* and fill in the chart
below with their food and drink order, as in the example.
Tip: جَوافة = guava.

نجوى: يا متر!

المتر: تحت أمرك، يا مدام.

نجوى: أريد سلاطة خيار بالنعناع لو سمحت.

المتر: نعم، والطبق الرئيسيّ؟

نجوى: سآخذ أسياخ الضأني.

المتر: طبقي المفضّل! مع الأرزّ؟

نجوى: لا، مع البطاطس المحمّرة.

المتر: وحضرتك؟

فريدة: ورق عنب للطبق الأوّل وبعد ذلك الدجاج المشويّ مع الأرزّ.

نجوى: ونحن الاثنان سنأخذ كعك مع سلاطة الفواكه للحلو.

المتر: حاضر يا مدام. والمشروبات؟

فريدة: نريد واحد كولا وواحد عصير جَوافة، من فضلك.

المتر: أنا آسف يا مدام. ليس عندنا جَوافة اليوم.

فريدة: إذاً سآخذ عصير منجا.

المتر: واحد كولا وواحد عصير منجا. تحت أمرك...

	Najwa	Farida
First course	cucumber and mint salad	
Main course		
Side order		
Dessert		
Drink		

8 ● Talk about it yourself تَكَلّم عَنها بِنَفسك

Now imagine you are meeting a friend, and are ordering lunch.
You want:
- stuffed tomatoes
- grilled fish with lentils (and rice)
- fruit salad with cream
- tea with mint

Your friend wants:
- carrot and onion salad
- chicken stuffed with figs and guava
- fruit salad with cream
- apple juice

Using the dialogue on page 36 as a model, write out the
conversation with the waiter. When you have finished, check your
answer with the model on the website.

_____

_____

_____

_____

_____

_____

_____

_____

_____

_____

Now repeat the conversation, but this time ordering your personal
favourites. You can use the menu on page 34 to help you decide.

1 How to get from A to B? Using the picture prompts, choose the correct combination of transportation from the three choices.

+ ٣

☐ بالباص ثمّ ماشياً
☐ بقطار الأنفاق ثمّ بالباص
☐ ماشيا ثمّ بقطار الأنفاق

+ ١

☐ بالسيّارة ثمّ بالقطار
☐ بالجمل ثمّ بالدرّاجة
☐ بالقطار ثمّ بالجمل

+ ٤

☐ بالطائرة ثمّ بالمركب
☐ بالطائرة ثمّ بالقطار
☐ بالباص ثمّ بالطائرة

+ ٢

☐ ماشياً ثمّ بالجمل
☐ ماشياً ثمّ بالحمار
☐ بالحمار ثمّ ماشياً

2 You have written a shopping list assuming you were catering for four people, but now it seems there will only be two of you. Rewrite your shopping list, cutting all the quantities in half, as in the example.

خمس برتقالات

عشر برتقالات
كيلو دجاج
نصف كيلو جبن
كيسان سكّر
لتر حليب
٢٠٠ جرام زبدة
أربع عُلَب بسكويت بالتين
بطيخة
زجاجتان زيت زيتون

3 Complete the crossword in English, using the Arabic clues.
One clue is completed for you.

ACROSS			DOWN	

ACROSS

طُرُق 1 (5)

شُرفة 3 (7)

مقليّ 5 (5)

نحوَ 6 (7)

مثير 8 (8)

نسينا 9 (2,6)

مساعد 14 (9)

مدخل 15 (8)

طعام 17 (4)

أعَدتُ 20 (1,8)

حُقول 21 (6)

يستمعون 23 (4,6)

كلمة مرور 25 (8)

حفيد 27 (8)

طبق اليوم 28 (4,2,3,3)

خيار 29 (8)

عائلة 30 (6)

شاهدتم 31 (3,7)

DOWN

واسع 2 (8)

طُيور 3 (5)

تذاكر 4 (7)

موهوب 6 (8)

نشتري 7 (2,3)

واحة 10 (5)

مكتب البريد 11 (4,6)

مفروم 12 (6)

يفضّل 13 (2,7)

أحياناً 16 (9)

جدّة 18 (11)

كرة اليد 19 (8)

ملاعق 22 (6)

غرفة الجلوس 24 (7,4)

أتذكّر 26 (1,8)

ثوم 27 (6)

4 Read Rashid's description of his work, and decide whether the statements below are true (صَحيح) or false (خَطَأ), as in the example.

أنا رئيس الحرس في أكبر محل لتجارة الذهب في العاصمة. عندي ثلاثة مساعدين.

أبتدئ عملي في السابعة والنصف صباحاً بزيارة مكتب الأستاذ شكري، رئيس المحاسبين، لأن الخزانة الرئيسيّة موجودة هناك. الخزانة في مكان سِرّيّ، وهو وراء صورة كبيرة للشيخ يوسف بن يوسف، صاحب المحلّ. لا أحد يعرف أن الخزانة وراء الصورة. أنا، والشيخ يوسف، والأستاذ شكري فقط نعرف ذلك.

بعد هذا أزور كلّ الأبواب والشبابيك لأتأكّد أنّها سليمة. وفي تمام الساعة التاسعة إلا ربعاً أطلب من المساعدين أن يفتحوا الأبواب.

خطأ	صحيح	
☐	☑	١ رشيد رئيس الحَرَس في محلّ.
☐	☐	٢ المحلّ هو لتجارة السجّاد.
☐	☐	٣ لرشيد ثلاثة مساعدين.
☐	☐	٤ يبتدئ رشيد عمله الساعة السابعة.
☐	☐	٥ خزانة المحلّ موجودة في مكتب رشيد.
☐	☐	٦ الخزانة وراء صورة كبيرة لصاحب المحلّ.
☐	☐	٧ صاحب المحلّ اسمه الشيخ يوسف بن يوسف.
☐	☐	٨ كلّ الموظّفين يعرفون مكان الخزانة.
☐	☐	٩ يتأكّد رشيد أن أبواب المحلّ وشبابيكهُ سليمة.
☐	☐	١٠ المحلّ يفتح الساعة الثامنة و٤٥ دقيقة.

5 Nur is talking about her work and hobbies. First, match the Arabic phrases with their English equivalents, and then decide which phrase fits into each gap in Nur's description, as in the example.

a	the university team	١	كبير المصوّرين
b	to enjoy it	٢	دَعوة خاصّة
c	chief photographer	٣	فَريق الجامعة
d	his hobby is his profession	٤	في شَبابه
e	nine medals	٥	للاِستِمتاع بِها
f	his height is two metres	٦	مُسلٍّ ومُفيد
g	entertaining and useful	٧	تسع ميداليات
h	private invitation	٨	طوله متران
i	in his youth	٩	هِوايَته هي مِهنَته

أنا صحفيّة في جريدة «صحّة الأسرة».
اليوم سأزور معرضاً اسمه 'الرياضة في
كلّ وقت'. سمعتُ أنّه معرض ــ٦ (g).
مدير المعرض أرسل لنا ــــ
لشخصين لزيارة المعرض. زميلي
محمد شاكر ــــ في الجريدة سيأتي معي. محمد شاكر
ــــ ، وكان من أفضل لاعبي كرة السلّة ــــ . هوايته
هي التصوير، واليوم ــــ ، وهذا شيء جميل!

أنا كنتُ كابتن ــــ في ركوب الدرّاجات، وعندي أربعة
كُؤوس و ــــ في خزانة زجاجيّة بجانب مكتبي. عندي
الآن درّاجة في البيت، ولكن للأسف، لا وقت عندي ــــ .

6 Finish this review by relating something interesting about your own work or hobbies, using phrases you have learnt in Units 1–6.

8 Clothes and colours
الملابس والألوان

1 Complete the table with the adjectives that describe colour or material, as in the example.

Arabic (feminine)	Arabic (masculine)	English
زَرقاء	أزرَق	blue
	جِلديّ	
		apricot (coloured)
سَوداء		
	صوفيّ	
لَيمونيّة		
		green
	بُرتُقاليّ	
		violet
	أبيَض	
ذَهَبيّة		
	رماديّ	
		red
قُطنيّة		
صَفراء		
	فِضّيّ	
		pink

2 Now describe these clothes using the picture and the English prompts, as in the example.

فُستانٌ قُطنيٌ أزرق ‹ـــــــــــــــــــــــــــــــــــ blue/cotton ١

ـــ black/leather ٢

ـــ orange/woollen ٣

ـــ red/cotton ٤

ـــ long/grey ٥

ـــ pink/leather ٦

ـــ old/violet ٧

ـــ new/silver ٨

3 Summer is here, so help Shadia put away her winter clothes and accessories. Put a tick next to the items that need to be packed away for the season, as in the example.

الجاكيت الكحليّ الثقيل ☐   الصندل المشمشيّ ☐

التي–شيرت الأصفر ☐   نظّارة الشمس ☐

الشال الصوفيّ الليمونيّ ☐   معطف المطر البنّي ☑

الشورت الأخضر ☐   القبّعة الصوفيّة الرماديّة ☐

الفستان البرتقاليّ الفاتح ☐   البلوزة القطنيّة البيضاء ☐
الفضفاض   الخفيفة

البوت الجلديّ الأسود ☐

4 What should we wear? Choose the most appropriate ending for each sentence or question, as in the example.

٦ هل لبستِ الفستانِ الحريريّ...	١ سألبس رباط العنق حين...
أ لتنظّفي أسنانك بالمعجون؟	أ أزور أمّي.
ب في حفلة منير؟	ب أذهب إلى المكتب.
ت في رحلة صيد السمك؟	ت أشاهد البرامج الرياضيّة
٧ سألبس البدلة الجديدة في...	٢ ألبس الصندل والشورت حين...
أ الاجتماع مع الوزير.	أ أنام بالليل.
ب المطبخ أو الحمّام.	ب أذهب إلى الشاطئ.
ت مصعد العمارة الجديد.	ت أركب الخيل.
٨ هل ستلبسون الجوارب الصفراء...	٣ يلبس حذاء الرياضة حين...
أ للسباحة؟	أ يلعب التنس مع أمينة.
ب لتلعبوا كرة القدم؟	ب يشرب الشاي أو القهوة.
ت لتشاهدوا المسرحيّة؟	ت يبحث عن كلمة المرور.
٩ ألبس معطفي الأزرق لَو...	٤ اِلبس البيجاما لأنّكَ...
أ جاء موعد العشاء.	أ ستزور جدّتك في المستشفى.
ب كنت أحجز غرفة في فندق.	ب ستأتي معي إلى السوق.
ت كان الجو باردًا.	ت ستنام بعد قليل.
١٠ نلبس الملابس القطنيّة الواسعة...	٥ يلبس نظّارته حين...
أ في شهور الشتاء.	أ يأكل الموز أو العسل.
ب في شهور الصيف.	ب يركب الدرّاجة أو الجمل.
ت في المكاتب والمحلات.	ت يقرأ أو يكتب.

5 Complete the table of verbs with doubled roots, as in the example.

Verbal noun	Past (he/I)	Present verb	Meaning
إعداد	أَعَدَّ/أَعدَدتُ	يُعِدّ	to prepare
		يُصَمِّم	
اِستِمرار			
		يَهتَمّ	to be concerned
	أصَرَّ/أصرَرتُ		
تَرَدُّد			to hesitate

6 Why is Hani hesitating about going to Widad's party?
Read what he says and answer the questions below.

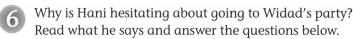

أحمد وأمين وقاسم يصرّون على أن
أذهب معهم إلى حفلة وداد يوم الخميس القادم، ويستمرّون
في الإصرار رغم ترّددي. في الحقيقة، أنا لا أهتمّ كثيراً بالحفلات.
أنا ليس عندي بدلة أنيقة لألبسها في هذه الحفلة. عندي فقط البدلة
الزرقاء التي اشتريتُها في الشتاء الماضي. كما أنّني سأحتاج إلى
قميص جديد. حذائي الأسود الجلديّ مثقوب. الجورب يخرج
منه أحياناً. الآن تعرفون أسباب ترّددي.

1 Who is insisting that Hani goes to Widad's party?
2 When is the party?
3 Why is Hani worried about his suit?
4 What else does he need to buy new?
5 What's wrong with his black leather shoes?
6 How does this affect his sock sometimes?

How many examples of verbs or verbal nouns with
doubled roots can you find in the speech bubble?
Underline them in the text.

Nabila is visiting her (maternal) aunt in Kuwait. She has
messaged this photo to a friend, explaining who is who. Read
Nabila's message and fill out the details in the table below.

هذه صورة لخالتي
فاطمة وهي تعيش في
الكويت مع عائلتها. فاطمة
هي المرأة التي تقف في وسط
الصورة، وتلبس الحجاب
والعباءة السوداء. زوجها
أحمد يلبس الثوب الأبيض
القطنيّ التقليديّ والشِماغ.

فاطمة عندها ثلاثة أطفال: بنتان وولد. البنت الكبيرة
اسمها ياسمين، وهي البنت التي تبتسم أمام فاطمة
في الصورة، لابسة البلوزة الورديّة والبنطلون الأبيض.
أختها الصغيرة، سارة، تلبس الفستان البنّي وتقف أمام
أبيها. الولد الصغير اللذيذ الذي يلبس الشورت والقميص
هو بُلبُل، ابن خالتي... حلو مثل السكّر! ☺ ☺

Name	Relation	Clothing
Farida	aunt (maternal)	hijab and black 'abaya' robe

8 🔵 **Talk about it yourself**   تَكَلَّم عَنها بِنَفسَك

You are visiting your (paternal) uncle, Danny, and his family in Canada.

You took this photo of his family. You are messaging the photo to your friend and explaining who is who.

Describe the photo, using Nabila's message on page 46 as a model.

You can use names and colours for clothing from your imagination.

When you have finished, check your answer with the model on the website.

_____

_____

_____

_____

_____

_____

_____

_____

_____

_____

Finish by finding a family photo of your own and describing who is who and what they are wearing in the photo. Write your ideas down; but also try saying them aloud, as if you were telling an Arabic friend about them.

Education and training
التعليم والتدريب

1 Choose a field of study from the box below and write it under the correct symbol, as in the example.

عِلم الاِجتِماع	اللُغات	الطِبّ	الهَندَسة
الجغرافيا	عِلم الكيمياء	عِلم الاِقتصاد	الرياضيّات
التَربِية الرياضيّة	الحُقوق	التَربِية الدينيّة	الموسيقى

٣ ـــــــــــــــــ   ٢ ـــــــــــــــــ   ١ ـ علم الاقتصاد

٦ ـــــــــــــــــ   ٥ ـــــــــــــــــ   ٤ ـــــــــــــــــ

٩ ـــــــــــــــــ   ٨ ـــــــــــــــــ   ٧ ـــــــــــــــــ

١٢ ـــــــــــــــــ   ١١ ـــــــــــــــــ   ١٠ ـــــــــــــــــ

2 After graduation, these eight young people found jobs in their fields of study. Choose the field and circle it, as in the example.

Samya teaches Maths. ١

التربية الرياضيّة / الرياضيّات / اللغـات

Iman is a lawyer. ٢

التربية الدينيّة / الجغرافيا / الحقوق

Justine is a social worker. ٣

علم الاجتمـاع / اللغة الصينيّة / علم الكيمياء

Mansour is an architect. ٤

التربية الرياضيّة / الهندسة / الموسيقى

Jamila is a surgeon. ٥

الحقوق / الطبّ / علم الاجتمـاع

Nadir works for an investment bank. ٦

علم الاقتصاد / اللغة الصينيّة / علم الكيمياء

Ismail is a dentist. ٧

الموسيقى / اللغة العربيّة / طبّ الأسنان

Jack works as a translator. ٨

التاريخ / الجغرافيا / اللغـات

3 Complete the present tense and the imperatives (instructions) for these verbs connected to learning, as in the example.

Imperative *(do!/don't!)*	Present verb	Past verb	Meaning
تَكَلَّمْ ! / لا تَتَكَلَّمْ !	يَتَكَلَّم	تَكَلَّمَ	*to speak*
		رَكَّزَ	*to concentrate*
		اِستَمَعَ	*to listen*
		نَسِيَ	*to forget*
		وَضَعَ	*to put/to place*
		أَكمَلَ	*to complete*

4   Every day, Madame Shushu, the manager of the Sultan's
    Palace Restaurant, briefs her staff and trainees. Read what
    she says and answer the questions below.

كل يوم، في تمام الساعة السابعة صباحاً، تجتمع مدام شوشو
سلطان، مديرة مطعم ʼقصر السلطانʻ، مع جميع العاملين في
مطعمها لتعطيهم أوامرها لهذا اليوم.

«لا تتكلّموا حتّى أنتهي، واستمعوا إلى تعليماتي جيّداً وركّزوا
على ما سأقوله لكم. ضعوا الزهور على الموائد، وافتحوا
الشبابيك. نظّفوا الملاعق والشُوَك والسكاكين جيّداً، ولا تنسوا
الأكواب. اِملأوا جهاز القهوة بالمياه المعدنيّة، وكذلك جهاز الثلج.
أغلقوا هواتفكم المحمولة قبل وصول الزبائن. رحّبوا بهم،
بدءاً من الباب، وحتّى جلوسهم على موائدهم. هل هناك أيّة أسئلة؟»

عادة، لا تكون هناك أيّ أسئلة لأن تعليمات مدام شوشو سلطان،
مديرة مطعم ʼقصر السلطانʻ لا تتغيّر أبداً. كلّ صباح، في تمام
الساعة السابعة صباحاً، نفس التعليمات، بنفس الترتيب.

1   What time is the daily staff briefing?
2   What is Madam Shushu's first instruction?
3   Where should they put the flowers?
4   What should they do to the cutlery?
5   What should they put in the ice-maker?
6   Why are there never any questions?

How many imperatives can you find in what Madame Shushu
says? Underline them in the text.

5 You are a new trainee in the Sultan's Palace Restaurant. You want to make a good impression and are writing an English list for yourself of dos and don'ts while listening to Madame Shushu's briefing. You have already written two notes. Complete the list below.

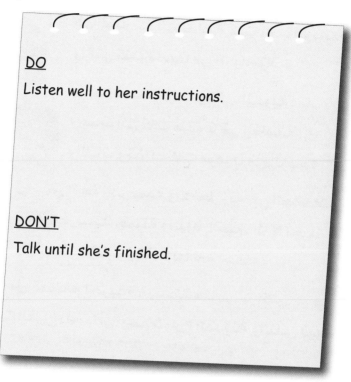

DO

Listen well to her instructions.

DON'T

Talk until she's finished.

6 Now match the Arabic phrases from the text with their English equivalents, as in the example.

a   never vary   ١ لتعطيهم أوامرهـا

b   beginning at the door   ٢ حتّى جلوسهم على موائدهم

c   to give them her orders   ٥ بنفس الترتيب

d   at exactly seven o'clock   ٣ لا تتغيّر أبداً

e   the same instructions   ٤ مع جميع العـاملين

f   until they sit at their tables   ٦ نفس التعليمـات

g   in the same order   ٧ في تمـام السـاعة السـابعة

h   with all the workers   ٨ بدءاً من البـاب

7 Tawfiq is talking about his educational journey in his native Marrakesh in Morocco. Read his story and complete the gaps in the summary sentences below.

أنا مغربيّ وأمضَيتُ طفولتي في مدينة مراكش.

في المدرسة الابتدائيّة كنتُ أحبّ الرياضة ولكنّي كنتُ ضعيفاً في الرياضيّات!

عندما ذهبتُ إلى مدرستي الثانويّة، وجدتُ أنّي كنتُ متفوّقاً في الفلسفة واللغات وكذلك كنتُ موهوباً في الرسم.

قرّرتُ أن أدرس اللغة الفرنسيّة والإنجليزيّة في الجامعة. أظنّ أن اللغة الفرنسيّة جميلة وسهلة التعلّم. أنا لا أجيد الكتابة والقراءة بالإنجليزيّة، لأنها لغة صعبة.

الآن أعمل كمصمّم لجريدة فرنسيّة هنا في مراكش. في وقت الفراغ، أحبّ أن أرسم شوارع المدينة والناس فيها.

١ في المدرسة الابتدائيّة كان توفيق ضعيفاً في _____.

٢ في المدرسة الثانويّة كان _____ في الفلسفة و _____.

٣ ووَجَدَ أنّه كذلك _____ موهوباً في _____.

٤ في الجامعة _____ توفيق اللغة الفرنسيّة و _____.

٥ يظنّ أن اللغة _____ سهلة _____ ولكن لا _____ اللغة الإنكليزيّة، خاصةً الكتابة و _____.

٦ الآن _____ كمصمّم، ويحبّ أن _____ شوارع المدينة.

8

● **Talk about it yourself**   تَكَلَّم عَنها بِنَفسك

Now suppose that you were born in Britain and spent your childhood in London. These are the details of your school and university days:

- At primary school, you liked reading but were weak in sport.
- At secondary school, you found you excelled in history and languages and were talented at music.
- At university you studied Arabic. You think it's difficult to learn, but you are good at reading and listening to Arabic.
- Now you work as a translator and also like to play the piano.

Using what Tawfiq says on page 52 as a model, write about your educational journey. If you are female, write in the feminine so that you become accustomed to using the correct gender. When you have finished, check your answer with the models on the website.

_____

_____

_____

_____

_____

_____

_____

_____

_____

_____

Finish by writing about your own educational journey and personal skills and talents. (If you are still at school or university, change what you say from past to present or future as appropriate.)

10 News and media
الأخبار ووسائِل الإعلام

1 Match the Arabic news topics to the symbols, for example ١h.

a

f

b

g

c

h

d

i

e

j

١ الرياضة

٢ السياسة

٣ الطبّ والصحّة

٤ الثقافة والفنّ

٥ الاقتصاد والمال

٦ الطقس والمُناخ

٧ الأخبار الدُوَليّة

٨ العُلوم والتكنولوجيا

٩ الأخبار المحلّيّة

١٠ المُجتمع

2 Now find the Arabic terms in the news topics above and write
them next to their English equivalents, as in the example.

_____	finance ٥	الصحّة	health ١
_____	science(s) ٦	_____	news ٢
_____	society ٧	_____	culture ٣
_____	politics ٨	_____	climate ٤

3 What are the plurals and meanings of these news- and media-related words? Write them after the singular, as in the example.

١ مَوضوع	topics	مَواضيع	_____
٢ مُشاهِد			_____
٣ مَصدَر			_____
٤ صَوت			_____
٥ قَناة			_____
٦ عامود			_____
٧ مُستَمِع			_____
٨ صَحيفة			_____
٩ بَرنامَج			_____
١٠ مُدَوَّنة			_____

4 Now fill in the gaps in these sentences to match the English in brackets, as in the example.

١ رأينا هذه __الصورة__ في قَناة «_____ الشعب».

(We saw this picture on the channel 'Voice of the People'.)

٢ أيُّها السادة _____، أهلاً بكم في _____

«_____ الخاصّ».

(Dear viewers, welcome to the programme 'My Private Palace'.)

٣ تَتَّفِق _____ على أنه نَصر لرئيس _____.

(The sources agree that it is a victory for the prime minister.)

٤ أكتب _____ أسبوعيّة عن _____ تغيُّر المناخ.

(I write a weekly blog on the topic of climate change.)

5 It's time for the weekly radio programme 'A Meeting with the People'. Look at the opening section of today's interview, and decide whether the statements on page 57 are true (صَحيح) or false (خَطأ), as in the example.

Tip: اِحتَفَلْتَ = you celebrated; يَخت = yacht.

– أيّها السادة المستمعون، أهلاً بكم في برنامج «لِقاء مع الشعب». ضيفنا اليوم هو الدكتور طاهر الأمين، رئيس الوزراء. مرحباً بك يا دكتور طاهر!

– أهلاً يا مدام وردة.

– يا دكتور طاهر، أرسلَ مصدر من مصادرنا صورة لقصر أبيض كبير وجديد، شبابيكه ذهبيّة، وفيه حمّام سباحة مشمشيّ على شكل قلب. مصادرنا قالت إنّ هذا قصرك.

– لا يا مدام وردة، هذا ليس قصري. هذا قصر زوجة وزير الزراعة.

– يا دكتور طاهر، رأينا في مدوّنة «عامود النصر» صورة لطائرة خاصّة لونها ليمونيّ فاتح. هل هي طائرتك؟

– لا يا مدام وردة، إنّها طائرة ابن وزير الصحّة.

– قرأنا في صحيفة «صوت الشارع» أنّك احتفلتَ في الأسبوع الماضي بشِراء يَخت فاخر جديد طوله ٤٠ متراً.

– لا يا مدام وردة، إنّه يخت ابنة وزير التعليم. أنا عندي درّاجة أركبها يوم الجمعة، وزوجتي تركبها يوم السبت، وأولادي يركبونها باقي أيام الأسبوع.

صحيح خطأ

خطأ	صحيح	
	✔	١ مدام وردة هي مذيعة برنامج «لقاء مع الشعب».
		٢ ضيف البرنامج اليوم هو رئيس الوزراء.
		٣ شبابيك قصر زوجة وزير الزراعة لونها فضّيّ.
		٤ ابن وزير الصحّة عنده قصر مشمشيّ على شكل قلب.
		٥ دكتور طاهر يكتب مدوّنة «عامود النصر».
		٦ ابنة وزير التعليم عندها يخت فاخر جديد.
		٧ زوجة دكتور طاهر هي وزيرة التعليم.
		٨ أولاد رئيس الوزراء يركبون الدراجة خمسة أيام في الأسبوع.

6 Join the Arabic adjectives with their nouns and the English meanings, e.g. **b ج ١**. Then complete the comparisons below using أكثر ('more') or أقلّ ('less') and a noun, as in the example.

a exciting/excitement	أ ضَعف		١ سَهل
b easy/ease	ب تَسلِية		٢ مُثير
c entertaining/entertainment	ت تَفاعُليّة		٣ ضَعيف
d interactive/interactivity	ث إتاحة		٤ مُتَوَتِّر
e weak/weakness	ج سُهولة		٥ تَفاعُليّ
f stressed/stress	ح إثارة		٦ مُسَلٍّ
g available/availability	خ تَوَتُّر		٧ مُتاح

١ البرنامج اليوم ‎أكثر إثارةً‎ (more exciting) من الأسبوع الماضي.

٢ هل اللغة العربيّة _____ (easier) من الصينيّة؟

٣ اللاعبون _____ (less stressed) من المدرّب قبل المُباراة.

٤ جدّتي _____ (weaker) بعد خروجها من المستشفى.

٥ كان الأكل العربيّ _____ (less available) هنا في الماضي.

٦ هل ألعاب الفيديو _____ (more entertaining) من الرياضة؟

Amjad is talking about how he and his family access the
media. Look at the additional vocabulary and read what
Amjad says. Then answer the questions.

Tip: شاشة = screen; مَعلومات = information; شَبَكة = net(work);
رَفيق = companion; نَظَر = (eye)sight; وَزن = weight.

أبي يُتابِع برامِج التليفزيون،

وجدّي يقرأ الصحيفة الورقيّة. أمّا عن نفسي،

فأنا ابن هذا القَرن. الشاشة التفاعليّة هي مصدر مَعلوماتي

المفضّل، والشَبَكات الاجتِماعيّة هي بيتي الثاني. هاتفي المحمول

هو رفيقي الذي لا يَترُكني، والحاسوب هو صديقي الذي يُساعِدني

في كلّ أموري. أظنّ أن حياتي أكثر إثارةً من حياة جدّي، كما أنّها

أكثر سُهولةً من حياة أبي، لأن المَعلومات أكثر إتاحةً الآن مقارنةً

بالماضي. نعم، أنا أقلّ تَوتُّراً من أبي، رغم أن نَظَري الآن أكثر

ضَعفاً، ووَزني زاد بسبب جلوسي أمام الشاشة

طوال النهار والليل!

1 How does Amjad's father access the media?
2 What about his grandfather?
3 What is Amjad's preferred source of information?
4 What does he refer to as his 'second home'?
5 What are his 'companion' and his 'friend'?
6 Why does Amjad think that his life is more exciting and
   easier than those of his father and grandfather?
7 What two effects on his health does Amjad say are a result
   of sitting in front of a screen all day and all night?

8 💬 ## Talk about it yourself   تَكَلَّم عَنها بِنَفسِك

Now talk about the media, using the information below and what Amjad says on page 58 as a model.

- Your father reads the newspaper every day.
- Television programmes are your mother's preferred source of information.
- As for you, the tablet computer (الحـاسوب اللَوحيّ) is your friend and companion that helps you with everything.
- You follow the social networks all the time.
- You think that your life is more entertaining than your parents' lives.
- But life is also more stressful compared to the past because information is available all day and all night.

When you've finished, check your answer with the model on the website.

_____

_____

_____

_____

_____

_____

_____

_____

_____

Finish by writing about how your own family accesses information and entertainment, perhaps also recording this as speaking practice.

unit

Climate and the environment
المُناخ والبيئة

1 Find and circle the words related to weather and climate in the word square. The words may read right to left or top to bottom. One is circled for you.

climate	winter	fog
weather	overcast	fine/clear
sunny	low	wind
wind	summer	dry
rain	storm	humidity
southerly	spring	clouds
snow	moderate	autumn

ل	ا	ق	ش	ض	ف	خ	ن	م	ك	س	ع
ة	ب	و	ت	ر	ة	م	ل	د	ت	ع	م
ة	ف	ص	ا	ع	ي	ا	ن	و	ج	ظ	ي
ع	ر	ك	ء	ا	ش	ض	ل	خ	ا	ن	م
ا	ي	ة	ب	و	ط	ر	د	ج	ف	ل	ح
ض	ح	ي	ص	ش	ق	ه	د	ة	ن	ر	ج
ر	ي	ت	ا	ي	س	م	ش	م	ة	ب	ع
ج	ل	ث	ط	س	ج	ط	م	س	ح	ي	ر
ه	ق	و	ح	ص	ر	ر	ظ	ح	و	ع	ي
س	ة	ض	ح	ي	ز	ل	ح	م	ئ	ا	غ
ح	ز	ب	ق	ف	ي	ر	خ	ي	ط	ب	ك
ب	ا	ب	ض	ه	ذ	ي	ب	و	ن	ج	ع

Rewrite the sentences about today's weather, firstly to refer to yesterday and then to refer to tomorrow, as in the example.

Tip: You will need to add the extra *alif tanwin* (أ) to masculine adjectives after كان ('was') or سَيكون ('will be').

اليوم الطقس معتدل. (Today the weather is mild.)

أمس كان الطقس معتدلاً .

غداً سيكون الطقس معتدلاً .

١ اليوم الطقس ممطر وغائم.

_____

_____

٢ اليوم الجوّ حارّ وجافّ.

_____

_____

٣ اليوم الرطوبة عالية.

_____

_____

٤ اليوم هناك رياح جنوبيّة خفيفة.

_____

_____

٥ اليوم السحب منخفضة والضباب كثيف.

_____

_____

3 Join the two halves of the sentences, for example: خ١.

أ فأنا أريد مقعدي بجوار الشبّاك.	١ إذا وجدنا شقّة على البحر...
ب فسنجد مكاناً نترك فيه السيّارة.	٢ إن زادت سرعة الرياح...
ت فسنطبخ البيض بدون نار.	٣ إذا حجزتِ تذكرة لي...
ث فستزيد سرعة المركب.	٤ إذا اشتريتَ خيمة لأحمد...
ج فهل ستشتري واحدة لي أيضا؟	٥ إذا أعجبتنا المسرحيّة...
ح فسنعود لنشاهدها مرّة أخرى.	٦ إذا وصلنا إلى الشاطئ مبكّراً...
خ فسنأخذها لعطلة الأعياد.	٧ إن ارتفعت الحرارة أكثر من ذلك...

4 Choose a word from the box to complete each of the phrases connected with the environment, as in the example.

تلوُّث	العَذبة	الهَواء	إعادة	الاِقتصاد
الرياح	حِماية	العُضَويّ	الشمسيّة	صديق

١ الطاقة __الشمسيّة__ (solar power)

٢ _____ التَدوير (recycling)

٣ طاقة _____ (wind power)

٤ _____ للبيئة (environmentally friendly)

٥ _____ في استخدام الطاقة (conserving use of energy)

٦ المياه _____ (fresh water)

٧ الغِذاء _____ (organic food)

٨ _____ الأنهار (river pollution)

٩ تَكييف _____ (air conditioning)

١٠ _____ البيئة (protection of the environment)

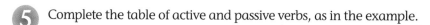

5 Complete the table of active and passive verbs, as in the example.

Past		Present		Meaning
Passive	Active	Passive	Active	
نُقِلَ	نَقَلَ	يُنقَل	يَنقُل	to transport
			يَصنَع	to manufacture
			يَبيع	to sell
			يُدير	to operate
			يَجِد	to find
			يَستَخدِم	to use
			يَأكُل	to eat
			يُعَبِّئ	to package

6 Using one of the verbs in the table above, how you would say the following in Arabic?

This machine is operated by solar power. ١

There is air conditioning ('air conditioning is found') in the hotel. ٢

Our fridge was manufactured in China. ٣

The food is packaged in metal tins (عُلَب مَعدَنيّة). ٤

Organic fruit was sold in the market. ٥

The waste (النُفايات) was transported by boat. ٦

7 Class 9 has written a blog about how their school in Qatar helps with the environment. Read what they say and complete the English summary points below.

مرحباً بكم في مدوّنة الصفّ التاسع!

هذا الأسبوع سنتكلّم عن البيئة، وكيف نساهم نحن في حمايتها.

الطاقة الشمسيّة

مناخنا مشمس طوال السنة. ولذلك، فإنّ كلّ الآلات وتكييف الهواء في مدرستنا تُدار بالطاقة الشمسيّة.

إعادة التدوير

الطقس حارّ جدّاً في إمارة قطر، خاصّةً في الصيف. التلاميذ يشربون مئات المشروبات التي تُعبَّأ في عُلَب معدنيّة يمكن إعادة تدويرها. عندنا أيضاً صناديق لإعادة تدوير الورق والزجاج.

خارج المدرسة

كلّ أسبوع نجمَع أكياساً كثيرةً من النفايات الموجودة حول المدرسة. تُنقَل هذه الأكياس لمصنع لإعادة التدوير.

ولا ننسى أن نقتصد في استخدام الماء، أغلى شيء في بلدنا الجافّ!

1 Our climate is _____ all _____.

2 All the _____ and the air _____ in our _____ are _____ by solar _____.

3 The _____ is very hot in the _____ of Qatar, especially in the _____.

4 All the drinks are _____ in _____ that can be _____.

5 Every week, we collect many _____ of _____ found _____ the school.

6 The bags are _____ to a _____ for _____.

7 We don't forget to _____ in the use of _____.

8

web ➜

🔵 **Talk about it yourself**   تَكَلَّم عَنْها بِنَفْسِك

Now imagine you are a pupil or a teacher at a school in Scotland
(إسكتلندا). Use Class 9's blog as a model and write something
similar about measures you are taking to conserve the environment.

- **Hydroelectric power** (الطّاقة الكَهرَمائيّة)
  Where you live the climate is rainy all year. In your school some
  machines and the heating are operated by hydroelectric power.

- **Recycling**
  The weather is very cold and snowy in winter. The pupils and
  teachers prefer to eat hot food. All the food is eaten on paper plates
  that can be recycled. You also have bags for metal cans and plastic.

- **Outside the school**
  Every week pupils help to collect rubbish in the streets around the
  school. The rubbish is transported to a factory for recyling.

When you've finished, check your answer with the model on the website.

_____

_____

_____

_____

_____

_____

_____

_____

_____

Finish by writing a blog about measures taken to conserve the
environment in your own institution, workplace or home.

unit 12 Health and happiness
الصحّة والسعادة

1 Write the names of the parts of the body next to the numbers, as in the example.

٦ ــــــــــــــــ		١ عين ـــــــ	
٧ ــــــــــــــــ		٢ ــــــــــــــــ	
٨ ــــــــــــــــ		٣ ــــــــــــــــ	
٩ ــــــــــــــــ		٤ ــــــــــــــــ	
١٠ ــــــــــــــــ		٥ ــــــــــــــــ	

2 Match the Arabic health-related words with their English equivalents, for example **e١**.

a blood pressure	١ وَزن
b tiredness	٢ بَدانة
c reduction/cutting down	٣ تَقليل
d allergy	٤ أَلَم
e weight	٥ ضَغط الدَم
f headache	٦ حَساسيّة
g diabetes	٧ حُمّى
h symptoms	٨ تَعَب
i pain	٩ مَرَض السُكَّر
j stress	١٠ أعراض
k obesity/corpulence	١١ صُداع
l fever	١٢ تَوَتُّر

3 What's wrong with me? Fill in the gaps in the ailments, using the picture prompts.

١ عندي ____ ألم ____ شديد في ____.

٢ أنا مُصابة بـألم ____ في ____.

٣ عندي برد و ____.

٤ عندي ____.

٥ أنا أشعُر بـألم في ____.

٦ عندي ____ من ____.

4 Two patients are chatting in a doctor's waiting room.
Read their conversation and decide in which order they
mention the topics below. The first is done for you.

المَريض ١: مساء الخير يا أستاذ.
الطقس حارّ الليلة، ويبدو
أن تكييف الهواء لا يعمل.

المَريض ٢: أنت على حقّ. التكييف
لا يعمل. الحرّ سيقتلني!

المَريض ١: وأنا أيضاً. وزني الزائد
يجعلني أشعر بالتعب
حين يكون الجوّ حارًّا هكذا.

المَريض ٢: وأنا أيضاً. أشعر بالتعب بسبب البدانة وارتفاع ضغط الدم.

المَريض ١: وأنا كذلك! كما أنّني أعاني كثيراً بسبب مرض السكّر.

المَريض ٢: غريبة! وأنا مثلك! كلّ هذه الأمراض تجعلني أشعر
بالتوتّر.

المَريض ١: أنا أدخّن أكثر حين أشعر بالتوتّر.

المَريض ٢: وأنا كذلك! يبدو أن الطبيب سيتأخّر. هل نذهب إلى
مطعم البيتزا في الطابق الأوّل؟

المَريض ١: فكرة رائعة! وبعد البيتزا نأكل آيس كريم بالقشدة...

smoking more under stress	☐	high blood pressure	☐
excessive weight	☐	air conditioning not working	☐
diabetes	☐	ice-cream with cream	☐
pizza restaurant	☐	hot weather	1
tiredness worse in heat	☐	lateness of doctor	☐

5 What's the matter? Choose the most appropriate ending for
each sentence, as in the example.

١ من المُحتَمَل أن تكون الأعراض
التي تشعر بها اليوم هي...

أ خضروات طازجة.

ب إيمايل من أخيك.

(ت) إنذار من جسمك.

٢ من المُرَجَّح أن التمرينات
الرياضيّة وتقليل الملح والسكّر...

أ ستسبّب البدانة.

ب ستكون مفيدة لكم.

ت ستسبّب سقوط الأسنان.

٣ خذوا المريض في رحلة إلى
الشاطئ لأنّه يحتاج إلى ...

أ قياس الضغط.

ب كلام الممرّضات.

ت الهواء الطَلَق.

٤ من الضروريّ يا أستاذ أن تُقلِع
عن المأكولات الدهنيّة لأن...

أ وزنك زاد كثيراً.

ب الصيدليّ سيسألك.

ت التدخين ضارّ بالصحة.

٥ لن تستطيع أن تستمتع
بحياتك إلا إذا...

أ حافظتَ على صحتك.

ب قرأتَ هذا الايمايل.

ت كنتَ عنيداً وغبياً.

٦ ينبغي علي أن أقلع عن
التدخين لأن أولادي...

أ يقرأون المجلات.

ب لا يحبّون الرائحة.

ت ينتظرونني في المطعم.

٧ الطبيب كان على حقّ! أشعر
أن حالتي تحسّنت منذ أن...

أ زاد وزني وسقط شعري.

ب جرّبتُ الكعك بالقشدة.

ت اهتممتُ بصحّتي.

٨ وزني الزائد يجعلني أشعر
بالتعب حين...

أ يكون الجوّ حارّاً.

ب أنام في سريري.

ت أشاهد برنامجي المفضّل.

6 Zeinah's friend, Nabila, has messaged her for some advice. Read Nabila's message and Zeinah's reply, and answer the questions below.

Tip: تَسَوُّس الأسنان = tooth decay.

قـالت لـي أمّـي إن مـن اللازم ألّا آكل حلويـات كثيرة لأن السكّر الزائد ضـارّ بـالأسنان كمـا أنـه يسبّب مرض السكّر والبدانة 😞. في الحقيقة أنا صغيرة السنّ ولا أشعر بـأي مرض. لا أريد الإقلاع عن أكلاتي المفضّلة مِثل الكعك والشوكولاتة. مـا رأيك؟ هل أنا على حقّ؟

يا حبيبتي نبيلة، من الأفضَل أن تسمعي كلام أمّك! أنت لا تشعرين بالمرض أو بـالألم الآن، ولكن من المرجّح أن السكّر الزائد سيسبّب لك مشاكل في المستقبل. ينبغي عليك يا صديقتي أن تقلّلي من الكعك والشوكولاتة، كمـا أن من المفروض ألّا تشربي الكولا بالسكّر. وأخيراً من الضروريّ أن تزوري طبيب الأسنان باستمِرار لِحِماية أسنانك من التَسَوُّس. وبعد ذلك من الممكن أن تستمتعي بـأسنان بيضاء قويّة وابتسامة جميلة! 😊

1 What is Nabila's mother telling her to eat less of?

2 Why is her mother telling her this?

3 Does Nabila feel ill?

4 What does Nabila not want to give up?

5 Does Zeinah agree with Nabila's mother?

6 What element of Nabila's diet does Zeinah think could cause problems for Nabila in the future?

7 What does Zeinah advise Nabila to cut down on?

8 Who does she advise her to see and why?

7 ● Talk about it yourself

تَكَلَّم عَنها بِنَفسك

You have received this message from your friend, Karim, asking for your advice about his health.

قـال لـي أبـي إن مـن اللازم ألّا أدخِّن سَجـائر إطلاقـاً لأن التدخين ضـارّ جِدّاً بالصحّة كمـا أنه يسبِّب تَسَوُّس الأسنـان ☹. فـي الحقيقـة أنـا صغير السنّ ولا أشعر بأي مرض. لا أريد الإقلاع عن التدخين. مـا رأيك؟ هل أنـا علـى حقّ؟

Reply to the message, giving your friend appropriate advice and using Zeinah's reply on page 70 as a model. When you have finished, check your answer with the model on the website.

_____

_____

_____

_____

_____

_____

_____

Finish by writing a short piece about what efforts you make to look after your own health, and what you might do to improve it.

1 Complete the table with the arts-related vocabulary, as in the example.

Plural	Arabic	English
أفلام	فيلم	film
	مُمَثِّل	
		play
راقِصون		
	رِواية	
أغانٍ		
		director
	شاعِر	
(plural as singular)		opera
	قِصّة	
مُؤَلِّفون		
	شِعر	
		musician
	رَقصة	
	مُغَنٍّ	
	بَطَل	

2 Read what different people have to say about their roles and circle their professions, as in the example.

١ هذه المسرحيّة من تأليفي.   مؤلّف / ممثّل / مخرج

٢ هذا الفيلم من بطولتي.   شاعرة / مخرجة / ممثّلة

٣ هل سمعتُم أغنيتي الجديدة؟   مغنٍّ / شاعر / راقص

٤ هذا البرنامج من إخراجي.   رَسّام / مخرج / مؤلّف

٥ أنا كتبتُ هذه الرواية.   ممثّلة / مغنّية / مؤلّفة

٦ رقصَتنا أعجَبَت الملك والملكة.   مغنّون / راقصون / مخرجون

٧ كانوا الأبطال في الأوبرا.   مخرجون / رَسّامون / مغنّون

٨ أشعاري مشهورة بين الشباب.   شاعرة / راقصة / مغنّية

3 Choose the film genre from the box that best fits each of these latest releases, as in the example.

تَسجيليّ	هَزليّ	رُعب	خَيال عِلميّ
حَربيّ	تاريخيّ	غَراميّ	بوليسيّ

تاريخيّ	Saladin Rides Again ١
_____	The Funnier Side of Comedy ٢
_____	Night of the Feasting Vampires ٣
_____	Water Features of Andalusia ٤
_____	Broad Street Murder Mysteries ٥
_____	Battle Cry Heroes ٦
_____	Love at Second Sight ٧
_____	The 07:05 to Mars ٨

4 Rewrite the sentences below to refer to a past habit or
preference, using the correct form of كان, as in the example.

أستَمتِع بأفلام الرُعب. (I enjoy horror films.)

كُنتُ أستَمتِع بأفلام الرُعب. (I used to enjoy horror films.)

١ جدّتي تُرسِل لي كتاباً كلّ أسبوع.

_____

٢ المخرج يُريد هذه الممثّلة في كلّ مسرحيّاته.

_____

٣ أجِد أن روايات نجيب محفوظ سهلة الفَهم.

_____

٤ إنّهم يغنّون ويرقصون في حفلاتهم.

_____

5 Now rewrite these sentences to refer to a hypothetical situation,
again using كان but with a future verb, as in the example.

شاهدنا المسرحيّة. (We saw the play.)

كُنّا سنُشاهِد المسرحيّة. (We would have seen the play.)

١ ذهبتُ إلى الحفلة الموسيقيّة.

_____

٢ قَرأت نادية القصّة كلّها.

_____

٣ اِستَمتعوا بالفيلم التاريخيّ.

_____

٤ اِستَمَعَ أبي إلى هؤلاء الشعراء.

_____

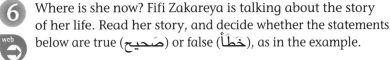

6 Where is she now? Fifi Zakareya is talking about the story
of her life. Read her story, and decide whether the statements
below are true (صَحيح) or false (خَطَأ), as in the example.

قصّة حياتي مثل فيلم سينمائيّ. أنا كنتُ أكبر ممثّلة في
العالم. كنتُ أحسن راقصة، وأشهر مغنّية. كلّ السيّدات
يَرقُصْنَ رقصاتي، والرجال يشاهدون كلّ أفلامي، والأطفال
يعرفون كلمات كلّ أغنية غنّيتُها، ويستمتعون بالاستماع
إليها في حفلاتهم. الشعراء والموسيقيون كانوا يُرسلون
لي أغانيهم لأسمعها وأغنّيها.
والمؤلّفون والمخرجون يريدونني
في مسرحيّاتهم لأكون بطلتها.

ولكن الآن، أعيش وحيدة في
قصري، مع الأشباح، ولا أحد يعرف
مَن أنا، ولا أحد يهتمّ بحياتي.

خطأ	صحيح	
☐	✔	١ كانت فيفي ممثّلة شهيرة.
☐	☐	٢ كانت أيضاً راقصة ومغنّية.
☐	☐	٣ كلّ الرجال كانوا يرقصون رقصاتها.
☐	☐	٤ عندها ثلاث أطفال.
☐	☐	٥ أُرسِلَت لفيفي أغانٍ لتسمعها.
☐	☐	٦ كان المخرجون يريدونها في مسرحيّاتهم.
☐	☐	٧ تعيش الآن مع عائلتها في بيت صغير.
☐	☐	٨ لا أحد يعرف الآن مَن هي.

7 Amjad is giving a short presentation about a film he saw recently. Look at the additional vocabulary and read what Amjad says. Then answer the questions below.

Tip: مَقبَرة = tomb; عالِم آثار = archaeologist; مومِيات = mummies.

> أوّل أمس شاهدتُ فيلم رُعب في السينما الجديدة القريبة من بيتي.
>
> كان الفيلم «ليلة المومِيات الحَيّة» وهو من بطولة النجم الشهير أحمد سليم. بطل الفيلم عالِم آثار في مصر والشخصيّات الرئيسيّة الأخرى هي مجموعة من عُلَماء الآثار (والمومِيات، طبعاً!).
>
> تدور القصّة حول اكتشاف مَقبَرة فِرعونيّة جديدة في جنوب مصر في بداية القرن العشرين، والأحداث المرعبة التي حدثَت بعد الاكتشاف.
>
> في الحقيقة استَمتعتُ بالفيلم ولكنّي وجدتُ أن القصّة كانَت مُضحِكة ولم أكُن مَرعوباً إطلاقاً. بل ضحكتُ طوال الفيلم كأنّه كان فيلماً هزليّاً!

1 When did Amjad see the film?
2 Where did he see it?
3 What type of film did he see?
4 What was the film called?
5 What was the job of the principal character in the film?
6 Who were the other main characters?
7 Where and when was the film set?
8 What discovery was central to the film?
9 Did Amjad enjoy the film?
10 Did he find it frightening?

8

💬 **Talk about it yourself**   تَكَلَّم عَنها بِنَفسك

Give a short presentation about a film you have seen recently, using the information below and what Amjad says on page 76 as a model.

- Last week you saw a historical film at a cinema in the town centre.
- The film was 'The House of Wisdom' (بيت الحكمة), written by the famous writer and poet, Bulbul Anwar.
- The hero of the film is the Caliph Al-Ma'moon (الخليفة المأمون). The other main characters are members of his family, especially his father, Haroon al-Rashid (هارون الرشيد), and learned men (عُلَماء) from around the Muslim world.
- The story concerns events in Baghdad in the 9th century, and how Al-Ma'moon founded (أسّس) the 'House of Wisdom'.
- You found the film exciting and interesting.
- You might have enjoyed it more but the historic language was sometimes difficult to understand.

When you've finished, check your answer with the model on the website.

_____

_____

_____

_____

_____

_____

_____

_____

_____

Finish by creating a short presentation about a film or performance you have seen recently.

1 Write the number of the picture next to the sentence or
question it represents below, as in the example.

☐ كلّ يوم أذهب إلى مكتبي بقطار الأنفاق.

☐ في شمال كندا المناخ عموماً بارد ومثلج في الشتاء.

☐ في المدرسة الثانويّة كنتُ متفوّقاً في العلوم والتكنولوجيا.

☐ أضيفوا بصلة مقطَّعة إلى الخليط.

☐ يشاهد ابني الأفلام على الانترنت ولكنّي أفضّل السينما.

☐ إذا ذهبنا إلى الصحراء، فَسننام في خيمة بين كثبان الرمال.

☐ أخي مراسل في قناة فضائيّة كويتيّة.

☐ من اللازم أن تقلع عن التدخين لأنه ضارّ جدّاً بالصحّة.

☐١ أين أقرب محطّة بنزين، من فضلك؟

☐ لن أحضر الحفلة لأن عندي صداع وألم شديد في أذنيّ.

Complete the crossword in English, using the Arabic clues.
One clue is completed for you.

ACROSS

1 أنيق (5)

3 سُحُب (6)

5 مُناخ (7)

8 مُصاب بـ (9,4)

10 هَزَليّ (5)

11 سُترة (6)

12 الآداب (10)

13 مَوهوب (8)

15 هي ابتَسَمَتْ (3,6)

16 الخَليج (3,4)

17 المُجتَمع (7)

19 مُذيع (11)

22 تطريز (10)

24 مُخرِج (8)

25 امتِحانات (5)

26 فضفاض (7)

27 مُشمِس (5)

DOWN

2 الطِبّ (8)

4 نحن نُواجِه (2,4)

6 هم نَقَلوا (4,11)

7 تَسجيليّ (11)

9 زَواج (8)

14 رِوايات (6)

18 زُوّار (8)

20 فُستان (5)

21 شُعَراء (5)

23 عِلم الأحياء (7)

3 Yasmine is talking about her daughter's recent wedding party.
Firstly, read the text; then try answering the questions below.

Tip: عَريس = bridegroom; عكس = opposite.

يوم الخميس الماضي احتَفَلنا بزفاف
ابنتي كريمة. نحن في موسم الشتاء،
ولكن الطقس كان مشمساً ودافئاً.

لبست كريمة فستان الزفاف الأبيض
التقليديّ. أمّا العَريس، إبراهيم، فلبس
بدلة سوداء أنيقة وَربطة عنق حمراء. وصل أبي بالطائرة من الخليج
لحضور الزفاف. للأسَف أمّي، جدّة كريمة، لم تحضُر معه لأنها كانت
مصابة ببرد شديد، فقال لها الطبيب إنّه من الأفضل ألّا تسافر.

في الحقيقة، كريمة هي عَكس إبراهيم تماماً. في المدرسة، كانت
متفوّقة في الرياضيّات والعلوم، وهي الآن طبيبة ناشئة. أمّا إبراهيم،
فكان يحبّ الآداب ويُجيد اللغات، وهو الآن مؤلّف وشاعر موهوب.

لن يسافرا الآن لشهر العَسَل لأنّ كريمة عندها امتحان إضافيّ، ويُكمل
إبراهيم روايته الأولى. ولكن في الربيع سيذهبان إلى روما لأسبوعين.
كان يوماً سعيداً جدّاً... كلّ الضيوف كانوا يَبتَسِمون طوال الحفلة.

1 When was the wedding celebration?
2 What are the names of the bride and groom?
3 What time of year was the wedding held?
4 What colours were the groom's suit and tie?
5 Who travelled from the Gulf to attend the wedding?
6 Who couldn't travel following advice from her doctor?
7 Do the couple have similar talents and professions?
8 Why aren't the couple going straight off on honeymoon?
9 Where and when are they going?
10 Does Yasmine think the guests enjoyed the wedding?

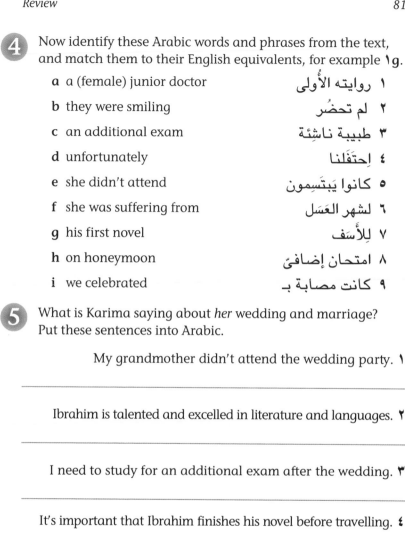

4 Now identify these Arabic words and phrases from the text, and match them to their English equivalents, for example ١g.

a a (female) junior doctor

b they were smiling

c an additional exam

d unfortunately

e she didn't attend

f she was suffering from

g his first novel

h on honeymoon

i we celebrated

١ روايته الأُولى

٢ لم تحضُر

٣ طبيبة ناشِئة

٤ احتَفَلنا

٥ كانوا يَبتَسِمون

٦ لشهر العَسَل

٧ لِلأَسَف

٨ امتحان إضافيّ

٩ كانت مصابة بـ

5 What is Karima saying about *her* wedding and marriage? Put these sentences into Arabic.

My grandmother didn't attend the wedding party. ١

Ibrahim is talented and excelled in literature and languages. ٢

I need to study for an additional exam after the wedding. ٣

It's important that Ibrahim finishes his novel before travelling. ٤

In spring, we'll go to Rome for two weeks. ٥

My mother was smiling throughout the party. ٦

6 Finish this review by describing a family wedding or a similar event you have attended, using Yasmine's description on page 80 for ideas, and including phrases you have learnt.

Answers to exercises

Myself and others

Activity 1
١ هي جَدَّتي ٣ هو حَمي ٥ هي حَماتي ٧ هو جَدّي ٩ هو خالي
٢ هو عَمّي ٤ هي خالَتي ٦ هو حَفيدي ٨ هي حَفيدَتي ١٠ هي عَمَّتي

Activity 2
٤ مِغار ٣ مضحك ٢ محبوب ١ رشيق
٨ عنيد ٧ موهوب ٦ رقيق ٥ نشيط
١٢ حكيم ١١ كريم ١٠ وفيّ ٩ ذكيّ

Activity 3
١ إنَّ حفيدتي موهوبة ولكنَّها عنيدة. ٢ إنّ زوج عمّتي فقير ولكنّه كريم جدّاً.
٣ إنّ صديقتي ذكيّة ومحبوبة ولكنّها كسولة قليلاً.

Activity 4
الاسم: ماجد محمّد؛ اسم العائلة: محفوظ؛ الجنسية: مصريّ؛ المهنة: مهرّج

Missing: Majid's address; Irrelevant: Majid lives with his grandmother.

Activity 5
٨ أمضَيتُ طُفولتي هنا. ٥ أختي موهوبة ولكنَّها ١ هو اسمه ماجد.
٩ إنّ حمي فقير ولكنّه كسولة. ٢ هل أنتُم لبنانيّون؟
كريم. ٦ كان لنا شقّة كبيرة. ٣ عندهم كلب أسود.
٧ أمّي كانت طبيبة أسنان. ٤ عُنوانها ٤٥ شارع النهر.

Activity 6
١ج؛ ٢خ؛ ٣أ؛ ٤ت؛ ٥ح؛ ٦ب؛ ٧ث

Activity 7
Al-Khaliji; Kuwaiti; south; Kuwait; born; I have; three sisters; father; farm; childhood; capital; Qatar; assistant; hotel; busy; happy.

Activity 8
(You'll find a model answer on the website for the final activity in Unit 1.)

House and home

Activity 1
٩ حَديقة ٧ مَطبَخ ٥ سُفرة ٣ غُرفة نَوم ١ سَطح
١٠ جراج ٨ صالة ٦ غُرفة جُلوس ٤ شُرفة ٢ حَمّام

Activity 2

٥ سَتَجِد الدش في الحمّام. ١ سَتَجِد السيّارة في الجراج.

٦ سَتَجِد مائدة الطعام في السفرة. ٢ سَتَجِد السرير في غرفة النوم.

٧ سَتَجِد السلّم في الصالة. ٣ سَتَجِد الأريكة في غرفة الجلوس.

٨ سَتَجِد العشب في الحديقة. ٤ سَتَجِد الفرن في المطبخ.

Activity 3

roofs ١٣ سُطوح	elevators ٧ مَصاعِد	bathrooms ١ حمّامات	
homes ١٤ مَنازِل	fridges ٨ ثَلاجات	houses ٢ بُيوت	
(dining) tables ١٥ مَوائِد	chairs ٩ كَراسي	rooms ٣ غُرَف	
entrances ١٦ مَداخِل	apartments ١٠ شُقَق	sinks ٤ أحواض	
	balcony(-ies) ١١ شُرُفات	kitchens ٥ مَطابِخ	
	clocks/hours ١٢ ساعات	cookers ٦ أفران	

Activity 4

a٣, b١, c٢, d١, e٣, f١, g٣, h٢

Activity 5

1 fish tanks; 2 construction and repair; 3 reasonable prices; 4 Eastern or Western style; 5 interior decorator; 6 internal and external stairs; 7 cleaning of swimming pools; 8 the best luxury woods.

Activity 6

٧ الشرقيّ	٥ ستائر	٣ الكرسيّ	١ السمك
٨ حمّام	٦ المكتب	٤ غرفة	٢ باب (المدخل)

Activity 7

Situation: middle of town/outside town. **Number of bedrooms:** one/two.
Guest room: no/yes. **Floor of apartment:** 4th/ground. **Garden/balcony:** no garden/garden or spacious balcony.

Activity 8

(You'll find a model answer on the website for the final activity in Unit 2.)

3 Work and routine

Activity 1

١٦ مُصَمِّم	١٣ عامِل	١٠ وَكيل	٧ سائِق	٤ خَبّاز	١ طَبيب
١٤ مَندوب	١١ صُحُفيّ	٨ مُساعِد	٥ طَبّاخ	٢ مُدير
١٥ طالِب	١٢ مُحامٍ	٩ بَنّاء	٦ حارِس	٣ فَنّان

Activity 2

طَبيب/أطِبّاء، مُدير/مُدَراء، حارِس/حُرّاس، وَكيل/وُكَلاء، عامِل/عُمّال، طالِب/طَلَبة

Activity 3

١ خَبّاز ٢ صحفيّة ٣ طبّاخون ٤ فنّانة ٥ أطِبّاء ٦ سائق

Activity 4 *(Answer below reads right to left.)*

٥ ،٢ ،٨ ،٣ ،٦ ،٤ ،١ ،٧

Activity 5

٩ منزلها	٧ تنظّف	٥ تكوي	٣ تأكل	١ تعمل
١٠ تطبخ	٨ ترتّب	٦ سيّارتها	٤ أبداً	٢ السادسة

Activity 6

a٦, b٣, c٧, d٢, e٤, f٩, g١, h٥, i٨

Activity 7

طارق أبو زيد، ١٩٨٠/٦/١٥، تونسيّ، ٤٤ شارع المِيناء ، كلّية إدارة الأعمال،
"ممتاز"، جامعة ليدن، التصميم بالكمبيوتر، وكيل للفنّانين، الشرق الأوسط،
المتحف الثقافيّ، جيّدٌ جدًا، متوسّط

Activity 8
(You'll find a model answer on the website for the final activity in Unit 3.)

4   Sport and leisure

Activity 1

١٠ كرة اليَد	٧ رُكوب الخَيل	٤ كرة السَلّة	١ الجولف
١١ رُكوب الدرّاجات	٨ ألعاب القُوَى	٥ المُلاكَمة	٢ السِباحة
١٢ الكرة الطائرة	٩ تنس الطاولة	٦ كرة القَدَم	٣ التنس

Activity 2

١ كرة ٢ الكرة ٣ ركوب ٤ تنس ٥ كرة ٦ صيد ٧ ركوب ٨ ألعاب

Activity 3

مُشاهَدة viewing/watching ش/ه/د؛ مَلعَب pitch/court ل/ع/ب؛ رُكوب riding
ر/ك/ب؛ تَصوير photography ص/و/ر؛ مُلاكَمة boxing ل/ك/م؛ مُدَرِّب trainer
د/ر/ب؛ سِباحة swimming س/ب/ح؛ مُمتِع enjoyable م/ت/ع؛ لاعِبون players
ل/ع/ب؛ مُفَضّل favourite ف/ض/ل؛ مُلاكِم boxer ل/ك/م؛ ألعاب games ل/ع/ب

Activity 4 *(features of the club that should be ticked)*

الجولف، تمرينات رياضيّة، مطاعم، ملاعب تنس، كرة السلّة، الاسكواش،
أنشطة عائليّة، إصطَبلات

Activity 5

١٠ مروان وإيناس	٧ إيناس	٤ إيناس	١ مروان
وكمال	٨ مروان وكمال	٥ مروان	٢ إيناس
	٩ إيناس	٦ إيناس	٣ إيناس وكمال

Activity 6
husband; likes; golf; watch; five; sofa; know; boring; two; three; small; players;
enjoyable; exciting; sport; sleep; advantage.

Activity 7
(You'll find a model answer on the website for the final activity in Unit 4.)

 unit

5 Travel and tourism

Activity 1
a٦، b٤، c٢، d٧، e١، f٨، g٩، h٣، i٥

Activity 2

٥ محطّة القطار   ٣ مركز الرياضة   ١ مكتب البريد

٦ مكتب السياحة   ٤ مركز الشرطة   ٢ مركز التسوّق

Activity 3

٨ بالتاكسي   ٧ بقطار   ٥ بالمركب   ٣ بالطائرة   ١ بالباص

٩ ماشياً   الأنفاق   ٦ بالجمل   ٤ بالدرّاجة   ٢ بالقطار

Activity 4

١ طائرة   ٢ جمل   ٣ درّاجة   ٤ سفينة   ٥ سيّارة   ٦ تاكسي

Activity 5

١ت؛ ٢ح؛ ٣ أ؛ ٤خ؛ ٥ب؛ ٦ث؛ ٧ج

Activity 6

مَشَيْتُ I walked م/ش/ي؛ شَعَرَتْ she felt ش/ع/ر؛ زُرْتُم you (pl.) visited ز/و/ر؛
نِمْتِ you (f.) slept ن/و/م؛ لَم يُغادِروا they didn't leave غ/د/ر؛ وَقَفْتُ I stood /
I stopped و/ق/ف؛ أَعَدّوا they prepared ع/د/د؛ لم أَجِد I didn't find و/ج/د؛
حَلَّ he solved ح/ل/ل؛ اِشْتَرَتْ she bought ش/ر/ي

Activity 7

١ ذَهَبَ سمير إلى الجامعة بالباص.   ٧ وَقَفَ الأسد ورائي، ولكنّي لم أشعُر
بالخَوف.

٢ رَكِبنا المركب إلى ميناء جدّة.

٣ كانَت الرحلة مُمتِعة ومثيرة جدّاً.   ٨ مَشَينا إلى الواحة ولكنّنا لم نشرَب
الماء من البِئر.

٤ هل شَعَرتِ بالعصبيّة على الطائرة؟

٥ ذَهَبتُ إلى السينما القريبة من بيتي.   ٩ هل أَعدَدتُم الحقائب واشترَيتُم
التذاكر؟

٦ زاروا أحمد في شقّته الجديدة.

Activity 8

١ ...طائرة   ٣ ...باص   ٥ النَخيل   ٧ جملاً   ٩ نُجوماً

٢ زُهور   ٤ جبالاً   ٦ ...بِئر   ٨ خيمة   ١٠ قَلعة

Activity 9
(You'll find a model answer on the website for the final activity in Unit 5.)

unit 6 — Food and cooking

Activity 1

١٦ جَزَر	١٣ نَعناع	١٠ بَصَل	٧ خُبز	٤ عَصير	١ دَجاج
١٧ تين	١٤ زُبدة	١١ لَحم	٨ خِيار	٥ ثوم	٢ جُبن
١٨ أُرزّ	١٥ تَمر	١٢ ماء	٩ بَيض	٦ سَمَك	٣ مَوز

Activity 2

٧ جزر	٥ بصل	٣ خبز	١ طماطم
٨ زبدة	٦ سمك	٤ تين	٢ ثوم

Activity 3

١ أريد كيلو لحم.

٢ أريد كيس بصل.

٣ أريد علبة سمك.

٤ أريد نصف كيلو جزر.   ٧ أريد كوب عصير برتقال.

٥ أريد ملعقة زيت.

٦ أريد ١٠٠ جرام زيتون.

Activity 4

١ سكّر   ٢ ليمون   ٣ بطاطس   ٤ بنّ   ٥ طماطم   ٦ تفّاح   ٧ منجا   ٨ لحم

Activity 5

١ تمر محشيّ

٢ بطاطس مهروسة

٣ جزر مبشور

٤ أسياخ لحم مفروم

٥ ليمون مخلّل

٦ كعك تقليديّ

٧ سلاطة الحمّص

٨ وَرَق عِنَب محشيّ

٩ بيض مسلوق

١٠ نعناع مقطّع

Activity 6

٣ ٢، ٧، ١٠، ١٢، ١٣، ١٧	٥ ٩، ١٧	١ ٣، ٥، ٦، ٧، ٨
٤ ٤، ٩، ١١	٦ ٢، ٤، ٥، ١٠، ١٦	٢ ١٦، ١٨، ٢١

Activity 7

First course: cucumber and mint salad/vine leaves. **Main course:** lamb skewers/grilled chicken. **Side order:** chips (fries)/rice. **Dessert:** cake with fruit salad (x2). **Drink:** cola/mango juice.

Activity 8

(You'll find a model answer on the website for the final activity in Unit 6.)

unit 7 — Review

Activity 1

١ بالقطار ثمّ بالجمل

٢ ماشياً ثمّ بالحمار

٣ بقطار الأنفاق ثمّ بالباص

٤ بالطائرة ثمّ بالمركب

Activity 2

خمس برتقالات، نصف كيلو دجاج، ربع كيلو جبن، كيس سكّر، نصف لتر حليب، ١٠٠ جرام زبدة، علبتان بسكويت بالتين، نصف بطيخة، زجاجة زيت زيتون

Activity 3

ACROSS: **1** ROADS; **3** BALCONY; **5** FRIED; **6** TOWARDS; **8** EXCITING; **9** WE FORGOT; **14** ASSISTANT; **15** ENTRANCE; **17** FOOD; **20** I PREPARED; **21** FIELDS; **23** THEY LISTEN; **25** PASSWORD; **27** GRANDSON; **28** DISH OF THE DAY; **29** CUCUMBER; **30** FAMILY; **31** YOU WATCHED. *DOWN:* **2** SPACIOUS; **3** BIRDS; **4** TICKETS; **6** TALENTED; **7** WE BUY; **10** OASIS; **11** POST OFFICE; **12** MINCED; **13** HE PREFERS; **16** SOMETIMES; **18** GRANDMOTHER; **19** HANDBALL; **22** SPOONS; **24** SITTING ROOM; **26** I REMEMBER; **27** GARLIC.

Activity 4

٩ صحيح   ٧ صحيح   ٥ خطأ   ٣ صحيح   ١ صحيح

١٠ صحيح   ٨ خطأ   ٦ صحيح   ٤ خطأ   ٢ خطأ

Activity 5 *(Answer below reads right to left.)*

(b) ٥ ،(e) ٧ ،(a) ٣ ،(d) ٩ ،(i) ٤ ،(f) ٨ ،(c) ١ ،(h) ٢ ،(g) ٦

Clothes and colours

Activity 1

blue أزرَق/زَرقاء؛ leather جِلديّ/جِلديّة؛ apricot مِشمِشيّ/مِشمِشيّة؛ black أسوَد /سَوداء؛ woollen صوفيّ/صوفيّة؛ lemon لَيمونيّ/لَيمونيّة؛ green أخضَر/خَضراء؛ orange بُرتُقاليّ/بُرتُقاليّة؛ violet بَنَفسَجيّ/بَنَفسَجيّة؛ white أبيَض/بَيضاء؛ gold(en) ذَهَبيّ/ذَهَبيّة؛ grey رَماديّ/رَماديّة؛ red أحمَر/حَمراء؛ cotton قُطنيّ/ قُطنيّة؛ yellow أصفَر/صَفراء؛ silver فِضّيّ/فِضّيّة؛ pink وَرديّ/وَرديّة

Activity 2

١ فُستان قُطنيّ أزرق   ٤ قميص قطنيّ أحمر   ٧ جيبة/تنّورة

٢ حِزام جلديّ أسوَد   ٥ معطف رماديّ طويل   بَنَفسَجيّة قديمة

٣ قُبّعة صوفيّة بُرتُقاليّة   ٦ صندل جلديّ ورديّ   ٨ قِلادة فِضّيّة جديدة

Activity 3 *(winter clothes and accessories that should be ticked)*

معطف المطر البنّي، القبّعة الصوفيّة الرماديّة، البوت الجلديّ الأسود، الجاكيت الكحليّ الثقيل، الشال الصوفيّ الليموني

Activity 4

١ب؛ ٢ب؛ ٣ أ؛ ٤ت؛ ٥ت؛ ٦ب؛ ٧ أ؛ ٨ت؛ ٩ب؛ ١٠ب

Activity 5

to prepare يُعِدّ، أعَدَّ/أعدَدتُ، إعداد؛ to design يُصَمِّم، صَمَّمَ/صَمَّمتُ، تَصميم؛ to continue يَستَمِرّ، استَمَرَّ/استَمَرَرتُ، استِمرار؛ to be concerned يَهتَمّ، اهتَمَّ/ اهتَمَمتُ، اهتِمام؛ to insist يُصِرّ، أصَرَّ/أصرَرتُ، إصرار؛ to hesitate يَتَرَدَّد، تَرَدَّدَ/تَرَدَّدتُ، تَرَدُّد

Activity 6

1 Ahmad, Amin and Qasim. **2** Next Thursday. **3** He bought it last winter and he's worried it isn't smart enough. **4** A shirt. **5** They have a hole in them. **6** His sock sometimes comes through the hole.

Activity 6 *(continued)*
Doubled roots that should be underlined (answer reads right to left):

يصرّون؛ يستمرّون؛ الإصرار؛ تردّدي؛ أهتمّ ؛ تردّدي

Activity 7
Farida: aunt (maternal); hijab and black 'abaya' robe. Ahmad: husband of aunt; white traditional robe and 'shimagh' headscarf. Yasmine: oldest cousin; pink blouse and white trousers. Sarah: middle cousin; brown dress. Bulbul: youngest cousin; shorts and shirt.

Activity 8
(You'll find a model answer on the website for the final activity in Unit 8.)

9 Education and training

Activity 1

١٠ الهندسة	٧ الجغرافيا	٤ علم الكيمياء	١ علم الاقتصاد
١١ علم الاجتماع	٨ الطبّ	٥ الحُقوق	٢ اللُغات
١٢ التربية الدينيّة	٩ الموسيقى	٦ التربية الرياضيّة	٣ الرياضيّات

Activity 2

٧ طبّ الأسنان	٥ الطبّ	٣ علم الاجتماع	١ الرياضيّات
٨ اللُغات	٦ علم الاقتصاد	٤ الهندسة	٢ الحقوق

Activity 3
to speak تَكَلَّمَ، يَتَكَلَّم، تَكَلَّم، لا تَتَكَلَّم!؛ to concentrate رَكَّزَ، يُرَكِّز، رَكِّز، لا تُرَكِّز!؛
to listen اِستَمَعَ، يَستَمِع، اِستَمِع، لا تستَمِع!؛ to forget نَسِيَ، يَنسَى، اِنسَ، لا تَنسَ!؛
to put/to place وَضَعَ، يَضَع، ضَع، لا تَضَع!؛ to complete أكمَلَ، يُكمِل، أكمِل، لا تُكمِل!

Activity 4
1 7AM. **2** Don't talk until I've finished. **3** On the (dining) tables. **4** Clean it well.
5 Mineral water. **6** Because Madame Shushu's instructions don't ever change.
Imperatives that should be underlined (reading in order from right to left):

لا تتكلّموا؛ استمعوا؛ ركّزوا؛ ضعوا؛ افتحوا؛ نظّفوا؛ لا تنسوا؛ املأوا؛ أغلقوا؛ رحّبوا

Activity 5
Do: Listen well to her instructions./ Concentrate on what she's telling us./Put the flowers on the (dining) tables./Open the windows./Clean the spoons, forks and knives well./ Fill the coffee machine and ice-maker with mineral water./Turn off our mobile phones./ Welcome the guests. **Don't:** Talk until she's finished./Forget the glasses.

Activity 6
a٣, b٨, c١, d٧, e٦, f٢, g٥, h٤

Activity 7

٥ الفرنسيّة؛ التعلّم؛	١ المدرسة؛ الرياضيّات ٣ كان؛ الرسم
يجيد؛ القراءة	٢ متفوّقاً؛ اللُغات ٤ دَرَسَ؛ الإنجليزيّة
٦ يعمل؛ يرسم	

Activity 8
(You'll find a model answer on the website for the final activity in Unit 9.)

10 News and media

Activity 1

a٣, b٩, c٥, d٨, e١٠, f٦, g٢, h١, i٧, j٤

Activity 2

١ الصِحّة   ٣ الثقافة   ٥ المال   ٧ المجتمع

٢ الأخبار   ٤ المناخ   ٦ العلوم   ٨ السياسة

Activity 3

١ مَواضيع topics   ٥ قَنَوات channels   ٩ بَرامِج programmes

٢ مُشاهِدون viewers   ٦ عَوامِيد columns   ١٠ مُدَوَّنات blogs

٣ مَصادِر sources   ٧ مُستَمِعون listeners

٤ أصوات voices/sounds   ٨ صُحُف newspapers

Activity 4

١ الصورة/صوت   ٣ المصادِر/الوزراء

٢ المُشاهدون/برنامج/قصري   ٤ مدوّنة/موضوع

Activity 5

✔٨, ✘٧, ✔٦, ✘٥, ✘٤, ✘٣, ✔٢, ✔١

Activity 6

١ج؛ ٢ ح؛ ٣ا ؛ه ؛ ٤خ؛ف ؛ ٥ت؛د؛ ٦ب؛c؛ ٧ ث g

١ أكثر إثارةً   ٣ أقلّ توتُّراً   ٥ أقلّ إتاحةً

٢ أكثر سهولةً   ٤ أكثر ضعفاً   ٦ أكثر تسليةً

Activity 7

1 He watches TV programmes. 2 He reads the daily newspaper. 3 Interactive screen.
4 Social networks. 5 His mobile phone is his 'companion' and his computer is his 'friend'.
6 Because information is more available. 7 His eyesight is weaker and his weight has
increased.

Activity 8

(You'll find a model answer on the website for the final activity in Unit 10.)

11 Climate and the environment

Activity 1

(Darker shade shows vertical words.)

ل	ا	ق	ش	ض	ف	خ	ن	م	ك	س	ع
ذ	ب	و	ت	ر	ة	م	ل	د	ت	ع	م
ة	ف	ص	ا	ع	ا	ن	و	ج	ظ	ي
ع	ر	ء	ا	ش	ض	ل	خ	ا	ن	م
ا	ي	ة	ب	و	ط	ر	ج	ف	ل	ح
ض	ح	ي	ص	ش	ق	ا	ر	ث	ن	ج
ر	ي	ت	ا	ي	م	ش	م	ة	ب	ع
ج	ل	ث	ط	س	ج	ط	م	س	ح	ي	ر
ه	ق	و	ح	ص	ر	ظ	ا	ح	و	ع	ي
س	ة	ض	ح	ي	ز	ل	ت	م	ئ	ا	غ
ح	ز	ب	ق	ف	ي	ر	خ	ي	ط	ب	ك
ل	ا	ب	ض	ه	ذ	ي	ب	و	ن	ج	ع

Activity 2

١ أمس كان الطقس ممطراً وغائماً.
غداً سيكون الطقس ممطراً وغائماً.

٢ أمس كان الجوّ حارًّا وجافًّا.
غداً سيكون الجوّ حارًّا وجافًّا.

٣ أمس كانت الرطوبة عالية.
غداً ستكون الرطوبة عالية.

٤ أمس كان هناك رياح جنوبيّة خفيفة.
غداً سيكون هناك رياح جنوبيّة خفيفة.

٥ أمس كانت السحب منخفضة
وكان الضباب كثيفاً.
غداً ستكون السحب منخفضة
وسيكون الضباب كثيفاً.

Activity 3

١ خ؛ ٢ ث؛ ٣ أ؛ ٤ ج؛ ٥ ح؛ ٦ ب؛ ٧ ت

Activity 4

١ الشمسيّة ٣ الرياح ٥ الاقتصاد ٧ العضويّ ٩ الهواء
٢ إعادة ٤ صديق ٦ العذبة ٨ تلوّث ١٠ حماية

Activity 5

to transport يَنقُل/يُنقَل/نَقَل/نُقِلَ؛ to manufacture يَصنَع/يُصنَع/صَنَعَ/صُنِعَ؛
to sell يَبيع/يُباع/باعَ/بيعَ؛ to operate يُدير/يُدار/أَدارَ، أُديرَ؛ to find يَجِدُ/
يوجَد/وَجَدَ/وُجِدَ؛ to use يَستَخدِم/يُستَخدَم/اِستَخدَمَ/اُستُخدِمَ؛ to eat يَأكُل/
يُوكَل/أَكَلَ/أُكِلَ؛ to package يُعَبِّئ/يُعَبَّأ/عَبَّأَ/عُبِّئَ

Activity 6

١ تُدار هذه الآلة بالطاقة الشمسيّة. ٤ يُعَبَّأ الغذاء في عُلَب معدنيّة.
٢ يوجَد تكييف الهواء في الفندق. ٥ بيعَت الفواكه العضويّة في السوق.
٣ صُنِعَتْ ثلاجتنا في الصين. ٦ نُقِلَت النُفايات بالمركب.

Activity 7

1 hot; year. 2 machines; conditioning; school; operated; energy.
3 weather; emirate; summer. 4 packaged; tins; recycled. 5 bags; waste; around.
6 transported; factory; recycling. 7 conserve; water.

Activity 8

(You'll find a model answer on the website for the final activity in Unit 11.)

12 Health and happiness

Activity 1

١ عين ٣ فم ٥ أسنان ٧ ذراع ٩ إصبع
٢ أذن ٤ أنف ٦ صدر ٨ يد ١٠ رِجل

Activity 2

a٥, b٨, c٣, d٦, e١, f١١, g٩, h١٠, i٤, j١٢, k٢, l٧

Activity 3

١ عندي ألم شديد في رجلي.   ٤ عندي صداع.

٢ أنا مُصابة بـألم شديد في أَذني.   ٥ أنا أَشعر بـألم في صدري.

٣ عندي برد وحمّى.   ٦ عندي حساسيّة من السمك.

Activity 4

1 hot weather; 2 air conditioning not working; 3 excessive weight; 4 tiredness worse in heat; 5 high blood pressure; 6 diabetes; 7 smoking more under stress; 8 lateness of doctor; 9 pizza restaurant; 10 ice-cream with cream.

Activity 5

١ت؛ ٢ب؛ ٣ ت؛ ٤أ؛ ٥أ؛ ٦ب؛ ٧ ت؛ ٨ أ

Activity 6

1 Sweet things. 2 Because too much sugar is bad for her teeth. 3 No. 4 Her favourite foods such as cake and chocolate. 5 Yes. 6 Excessive sugar. 7 Cake, chocolate and sugary cola. 8 A dentist to advise her how to protect her teeth from decay.

Activity 7

(You'll find a model answer on the website for the final activity in Unit 12.)

unit 13 Arts and cinema

Activity 1

film فيلم/أَفلام؛ actor مُمثّل/مُمثّلون؛ play مسرحيّة/مسرحيّات؛ dancer راقِص/راقِصون؛ novel رواية/روايات؛ song أُغنية/أَغانٍ؛ director مُخرج/مُخرجون؛ poet شاعر/شُعَراء؛ opera أوبرا؛ story قِصّة/قِصَص؛ author مُؤَلّف/مُؤَلّفون؛ poem/poetry شِعر/أَشعار؛ musician موسيقيّ/موسيقيّون؛ dance رَقصة/رقصات؛ singer مُغنٍ/مُغنّون؛ hero بَطَل/أَبطال

Activity 2

٧ مغنّون	٥ مُؤَلّفة	٣ مغنٍّ	١ مؤلّف
٨ شاعرة	٦ راقصون	٤ مخرج	٢ ممثّلة

Activity 3

٧ غراميّ	٥ بوليسيّ	٣ رُعب	١ تاريخيّ
٨ خيال علميّ	٦ حربيّ	٤ تسجيليّ	٢ هزليّ

Activity 4

١ كانت جدّتي تُرسِل لي كتاباً كلّ أسبوع.

٢ كان المخرج يُريد هذه الممثّلة في كلّ مسرحيّاته.

٣ كنتُ أَجِد أَن روايات نجيب محفوظ سهلة الفَهم.

٤ كانوا يغنّون ويرقصون في حفلاتهم.

Activity 5

١ كنتُ سأذهب إلى الحفلة الموسيقيّة.   ٣ كانوا سيستمتعون بالفيلم التاريخيّ.

٢ كانت نادية ستقرأ القصّة كلّها.   ٤ كان أبي سيستمع إلى هؤلاء الشعراء.

Activity 6

٧ خطأ	٥ صحيح	٣ خطأ	١ صحيح
٨ صحيح	٦ صحيح	٤ خطأ	٢ صحيح

Activity 7

1 The day before yesterday. 2 In the new cinema near his house. 3 Horror. 4 'The Night of the Living Mummies'. 5 An archaeologist. 6 A group of archaeologicals (and the mummies!). 7 In the South of Egypt at the beginning of the 20th century. 8 A new pharaonic tomb. 9 Yes. 10 Not at all (he found it funny).

Activity 8

(You'll find a model answer on the website for the final activity in Unit 13.)

14 Review

Activity 1 *(Answer below reads right to left.)*

٨ ،١ ،٥ ،٤ ،٩ ،٢ ،٦ ،٣ ،٧ ،١٠

Activity 2

ACROSS: 1 SMART; 3 CLOUDS; 5 CLIMATE; 8 SUFFERING FROM; 10 COMIC; 11 JACKET; 12 LITERATURE; 13 TALENTED; 15 SHE SMILED; 16 THE GULF; 17 SOCIETY; 19 BROADCASTER; 22 EMBROIDERY; 24 DIRECTOR; 25 EXAMS; 26 FLOWING; 27 SUNNY. *DOWN:* 2 MEDICINE; 4 WE FACE; 6 THEY TRANSPORTED; 7 DOCUMENTARY; 9 MARRIAGE; 14 NOVELS; 18 VISITORS; 20 DRESS; 21 POETS; 23 BIOLOGY.

Activity 3

1 Last Thursday. 2 Karima and Ibrahim. 3 Winter. 4 Black suit and red tie. 5 Yasmine's father (Karima's grandfather). 6 Yasmine's mother (Karima's grandmother). 7 No, they're opposite types (Karima is good at mathematics and science; Ibrahim at literature and languages). 8 Because Karima has an exam and Ibrahim needs to complete his first novel. 9 To Rome in the spring. 10 Yes, they were smiling all the time.

Activity 4

a٣, b٥, c٨, d٧, e٢, f٩, g١, h٦, i٤

Activity 5

١ لم تحضر جدّتي حفلة الزفاف.

٢ إبراهيم موهوب وكان متفوّقاً في الآداب واللغات.

٣ من الضروريّ أن أدرس لامتحان إضافيّ بعد الزفاف.

٤ من المهمّ أن يُكمل إبراهيم روايته قبل السفر.

٥ في الربيع، سنذهب إلى روما لأسبوعين.

٦ كانت أمّي تبتسم طوال الحفلة.

Activity 6

(This is the final activity and is based on your personal experience. Try to check your description with an Arabic-speaking teacher or friend.)